pred	faulty predication	**40**
quot	quotation marks placed improperly in relation to punctuation mark **80, 81, 82**	
ref	faulty pronoun reference	**24**
rep	careless repetition	**47**
restr	punctuate a restrictive clause properly	**65**
sp	spelling error	
title	improper format of title for published work	**83, 84**
trite	trite expression	**44**
vb	improper form of verb	**33**
wdy	wordy sentence	**46**
ww	wrong word	**40**

PROOFREADERS' MARKS

⌒ close up space

⌐ delete

⌐ delete and close up space

separate with a space

∧ insert here what is indicated in the margin

¶ start new paragraph

no ¶ no paragraph; run in with previous paragraph

⊙ / insert period   (cap) use capital letter here

∧ / insert comma   (lc) use lowercase letter here

; / insert semicolon   (ital) set in italic type

: / insert colon   (rom) set in roman type

$\frac{1}{M}$ / insert em dash   (sc) set in small capitals

$\frac{1}{M}$/$\frac{1}{M}$ insert pair of em dashes   (bf) set in boldface type

= / insert hyphen   (tr) transpose letters

∨ / insert apostrophe   or words

The
Little
English
Handbook

The Little English Handbook

Choices and Conventions

Sixth Edition

Edward P. J. Corbett
The Ohio State University

Sheryl L. Finkle
Northern Illinois University

HarperCollins*Publishers*

This book is dedicated to all our students over the years, whose written prose sometimes mystified us, often enlightened us, and invariably beguiled us. Bless them all.

Executive Editor: Constance Rajala
Development Editor: Hope Rajala
Project Editor: Karen Trost
Design Supervisor/Cover Design: Dorothy Bungert
Production Assistant: Linda Murray
Compositor: Better Graphics, Inc.
Printer and Binder: Courier Corporation
Cover Printer: New England Book Components, Inc.

Adapted excerpts from *Structural Essentials of English* by Harold Whitehall, copyright, 1954, © 1956 by Harcourt Brace Jovanovich, Inc. Reprinted by permission of the publisher.

The Little English Handbook, Sixth Edition
Copyright © 1992 by HarperCollins Publishers Inc.

Library of Congress Cataloging-in-Publication Data

Corbett, Edward P. J.
    The little English handbook   :   choices and conventions /
  Edward P. J. Corbett, Sheryl L. Finkle. — 6th ed.
      p.   cm.
    Includes index.
    ISBN 0-673-46048-7 (student edition)
    ISBN 0-673-46544-6 (teacher edition)
    1. English language—Rhetoric—Handbooks, manuals, etc.
  2. English language—Usage—Handbooks, manuals, etc.   I.
  Finkle, Sheryl L.   II. Title.
  PE1408.C587   1992
808'.042—dc20   91-14331
                                                          CIP

      93 94 9 8 7 6 5 4 3

CONTENTS

PREFACE

The Little English Handbook is designed to serve as a guide on basic matters of grammar, style, paragraphing, punctuation, and mechanics for those engaged in writing public prose. By "public prose," we mean that dialect of written English most commonly used in the newspapers, magazines, and books that the majority of educated native speakers read. This dialect ranges in style from the formal to the casual, from the literary to the colloquial. But because public prose has to be intelligible to a general audience, it avoids the esoteric vocabulary of various professional, regional, and social groups, and it observes the rules of grammar as taught in the schools.

The use of the term *public prose* is not intended to disparage the other current dialects, most of which serve well the needs of some of the people all of the time and all of the people some of the time. Obviously, spoken English, with its own wide range of professional, regional, and social dialects, serves the needs of more people more often than written English does. However, despite the primacy of the spoken language, there are occasions when many, if not most, native speakers must use the written language in order to record or communicate their thoughts, needs, and feelings. It is for those occasions that this handbook was prepared.

A Handbook for Common Problems

Ever since the first edition of this handbook, we have concentrated on those matters of grammar, style, paragraphing, punctuation, and mechanics that, from years of experience in reading student papers and responding to telephone queries from people in business and the professions, we know to be the most common and persistent problems in the expressive part of the writing process. For answers to the larger and more subtle problems in writing prose, you will have to consult one of the larger handbooks. We do not, for instance, provide guidance in all the uses of the comma; some of these uses are never or only seldom a problem for writers. Instead, we deal only with those half dozen conventions of the comma that are most often ignored or misused and that are most crucial for the preservation of clarity. If you master these six uses, you can rest assured that there are no really serious mistakes that you can make in the use (or the omission) of the comma.

Choices and Conventions

The subtitle of this handbook, *Choices and Conventions,* reflects our approach. Some of the principles governing the system of writing have been established by conventions; others represent recommendations from a number of options. Accordingly, in most cases, we have stated the guiding principle in definite, unequivocal terms. We are the first to concede, however, that in matters of language, there should be no absolute prescriptions or proscriptions. Where choices are available, you must be guided in making your selection by a consideration of the subject matter, occasion, desired effect, and audience. But in our experience, those who need the guidance of a handbook want a simple, straightforward answer to their query.

Priorities in the Writing Process

By concentrating on matters of grammar, style, paragraphing, punctuation, and mechanics, we do not wish to imply that these are the most important concerns of "good writing." What is most necessary for effective communication is the substance, originality, and sophistication of your thoughts and the ability to organize your thoughts in a unified, coherent way. Inept articulation of your thoughts is often a reflection of inept processes of invention and organization. Careless expression stems ultimately from careless thinking. Observance of the "basics" treated in this handbook will not guarantee that your prose will be interesting to read or worth reading, but observance of the fundamental conventions of the writing system will at least guarantee that your prose can be read. Readable prose is no mean achievement. The next achievement to strive for is to write prose that others will want to read.

Acknowledgments

Every textbook designed for classroom use profits from criticisms and suggestions of experienced, knowledgeable teachers. The list of teachers who reviewed the manuscript of the first edition, of those who provided detailed critiques of subsequent editions, and of those who buttonholed us at conventions to offer us their suggestions for improving the text would be a long one indeed. We resort here to a collective word of appreciation to those teachers whose suggestions greatly improved previous editions. But we do want to acknowledge by name the teachers who were commissioned to review the manuscript of the sixth edition and who provided helpful suggestions: William L. Davis, University of Texas-Pan American; Richard R. Holmes, Culver Stockton College; Kenneth Christopherson, Pacific

Lutheran University; George P. E. Meese, Eckerd College; Joanne M. Hayes, Greenfield Community College; Dr. John O. White, California State University at Fullerton; Molly Frances Moore, University of Vermont; Noreen Herzfeld, St. John's University; and Victoria Carlson-Casaregola, University of Wisconsin at Oshkosh.

Dr. Sheryl Finkle, who was taken aboard as a coauthor of this sixth edition, reviewed hundreds of student papers to garner new examples of questionable sentences for the Grammar, Style, Punctuation, and Mechanics sections of the handbook. Being a relatively young teacher, she was able to provide a fresh perspective on many of the matters that are dealt with in this book.

The author of any textbook also owes a great debt of gratitude to many people on the staff of his or her publisher—not only the people in the Editorial department but also the people in the Design, the Production, and the Promotion departments. If we were to acknowledge by name all those on the staff of HarperCollins to whom we are indebted, the list of acknowledgments would extend for several more inches. But we want to single out for special mention here a few people who have been involved in the preparation and production of this and previous editions of *The Little English Handbook:* Anne Smith, Constance Rajala, Hope Rajala, Karen Trost, Dorothy Bungert, and Linda Murray. They are the ones to be credited with the merits of the book. We alone are responsible for any instances of ineptitude or wrongheadedness in the text.

Edward P. J. Corbett
Sheryl L. Finkle

LEGEND

Some of the conventions presented in this handbook, especially those having to do with punctuation, are illustrated with graphic models using these symbols:

A word inside the box designates a particular part of speech, e.g., ⬚noun⬚ .

$$\boxed{} = \text{word}$$

A phrase is a meaningful combination of two or more words that does not constitute a clause.

$$\underline{} = \text{phrase}$$

The following abbreviations on the horizontal line designate a particular kind of phrase, e.g., $\underline{}^{\text{prep.}}$.

- **prep.** = prepositional phrase (**on the bus**)
- **part.** = participial phrase (**having ridden on the bus**)
- **ger.** = gerund phrase (**riding on the bus** pleased him)
- **inf.** = infinitive phrase (he wanted **to ride on the bus**)

An independent clause, sometimes referred to as a main clause, can stand by itself as a grammatically complete sentence, e.g., **He rode on the bus.** The vertical line indicates the separation of subject from predicate.

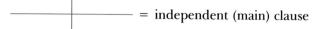 = independent (main) clause

A dependent clause, sometimes referred to as a subordinate clause, cannot stand by itself as a grammatically complete sentence.

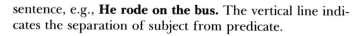 = dependent (subordinate) clause

The following abbreviations printed above the first vertical line designate a particular kind of dependent clause, e.g.,

noun = noun clause (He claimed **that he rode on the bus.**)

adj. = adjective clause (The man **who rode on the bus** was pleased.)

adv. = adverb clause (He was late **because he rode on the bus.**)

noun

= dependent (subordinate) noun clause

FORMAT OF MANUSCRIPT

In preparing the final draft of a manuscript, follow the specific directions about format given by your instructor or editor. However, if no specific directions are given, you can be confident that the format of your manuscript will be acceptable if you observe the following conventions:

10 Write on one side of the paper only.

11 Double-space the lines of prose, whether you handwrite or typewrite.

A manuscript submitted to an editor for consideration must be typewritten and double-spaced.

12 Preserve a left-hand and a right-hand margin.

3

13 Put the title of your paper at the top of the first page of your manuscript—even though you may have put the title on a cover sheet.

See the end of **84** for instructions about how to set down the title of your paper.

14 Number all pages at the top of the page—in the middle or at the right-hand margin.

15 Secure your manuscript with a paper clip.

Many editors will not even read a manuscript that is stapled together.

16 Use the proper kind of paper.

If you typewrite your manuscript, use white, unlined, opaque paper. If you handwrite your manuscript, use white, lined theme paper.

17 If you use a word processor, ask your instructor or editor for special directions or limitations.

Ask whether it is permissible (1) to use a word processor, and (2) to submit a paper that is produced on something less than a letter-quality printer.

GRAMMAR

Grammar may be defined as the study of how a language "works"—a study of how the structural system of a language combines with a vocabulary to convey meaning. When we study a foreign language in school, we must study both **vocabulary** and **grammar**, and until we can put the two together, we cannot translate the language. Sometimes we know the meaning of every word in a foreign-language sentence, and yet we cannot translate the sentence because we cannot figure out its grammar. On the other hand, we sometimes can figure out the grammar of the foreign-language sentence, but because we do not know the meaning of one or more words in the sentence, we still cannot translate the sentence.

If you heard or read this sequence of words, you might notice that the sequence bears a marked resemblance to an English sentence.

> The porturbs in the brigger torms have tanted the makrets' rotment brokly.

Although many words in that sequence would be unfamiliar, you would detect that the sequence had the structure of the kind of English sentence that makes a statement, and you might further surmise that this kind of statement pattern was one that said that *porturbs* (whoever they are) had done something to *rotment* (whatever that is); or, to put it another way, that *porturbs* was the subject of the sentence, that *have tanted* was the predicate verb, and that *rotment* was the object of that verb, the receiver of the action performed by the doer, *porturbs*. How were you able to make that much "sense" out of that sequence of strange words? You were able to detect that much sense by noting the following structural signals:

● **Function words:**

The three occurrences of the article **the**, the preposition **in**, and the auxiliary verb **have**.

● **Inflections and affixes:**

The **-s** added to the nouns to form the plural, the **-er** added to adjectives to form the comparative degree, the **-ed** added to verbs to form the past tense or the past participle, the **-s'** added to nouns to form the plural possessive case, the affix **-ment** added to certain words to form an abstract noun, and the **-ly** added to adjectives to form adverbs.

● **Word order:**

The basic pattern of a statement or declarative sentence in English is S (subject) + V (verb) + C (complement) or NP (noun phrase) + VP (verb phrase). In the sequence, **The porturbs in the brigger torms** appears to be the S or NP part of the sentence and **have tanted the makrets' rotment brokly** the VP part of the sentence (**have tanted** being the V and **the makrets' rotment brokly** being the C).

● **Intonation (stress, pitch, and juncture):**

If the sequence were spoken aloud, you would detect that the sequence had the intonational pattern of the declarative sentence in spoken English.

● **Punctuation and mechanics:**

If the sequence were written (as it is here), you would observe that it began with a capital letter and ended with a period, two typographical devices that signal a statement in written English.

You would be able to read a relational sense or structural meaning into the string of nonsense words simply by observing the grammatical devices of **inflections**, **function words**, **word order**, and **intonation** (if spoken) or **punctuation** (if written). Now, if you had a dictionary that defined such words as **porturb**, **brig**, **torm**, **tant**, **makret**, **rotment**, and **brok**, you would be able to translate the full meaning of the sentence. But by observing the structural or grammatical devices alone, you could perceive that the sequence of words

> The porturbs in the brigger torms have tanted the makrets' rotment brokly.

exactly matches the structure of an English sentence like this one:

> The citizens in the larger towns have accepted the legislators' commitment enthusiastically.

What you have been concentrating on is the *grammar* of the sentence, and it is in this structural sense that the term *grammar* is used in the section that follows.

This section on grammar deals with those devices of *inflection, function words,* and *word order* that makes it possible for written sentences to convey to readers, clearly and unmistakably, a writer's intended meaning. We are not concerned here with *intonation,* because this handbook deals only with the written language. In a later section, we shall consider the fourth grammatical device of written English, *punctuation.*

20 Apostrophe for Possessive

Use an apostrophe for the possessive case of the noun.

| noun | 's | | noun | s' |

poet's   **poets'**

Here are some guidelines for forming the possessive case of the English noun:

(a) As the diagrams above indicate, most English nouns form the possessive case with **'s** (singular) or **s'** (plural). An alternative form of the possessive case consists of an **of** phrase: **the commands of the general** (instead of **the general's commands**).

(b) Nouns that form their plural in ways other than by adding an **s** form their possessive in the plural by adding **'s** to the plural of the noun: **woman's/women's**, **man's/men's**, **child/children's**, **ox's/oxen's**, **deer's/deer's**, **mouse's/mice's**.

(c) Some writers simply add an apostrophe to form the possessive case of singular nouns ending in **s**:

the goddess' fame

the alumnus' contribution

Keats' odes

Dickens' novels

However, other writers add the usual **'s** to form the possessive case of such nouns: **goddess's**, **alumnus's**, (plural **alumni's**), **Keats's**, **Dickens's**. Take your choice, but be consistent.

(d) The rules for forming the possessive case of pairs of nouns are as follows: (1) in the case of *joint* possession, add **'s** only to the second member of the pair: **John and Mary's**

mother, **the brother and sister's car**, and (2) in the case of *individual* possession, add **'s** to each member of the pair: **the boy's and girl's bedrooms, John's and Mary's tennis rackets, the men's and women's locker rooms**.

(e) Form the possessive case of group nouns or compound nouns by adding **'s** to the end of the unit: **commander in chief's, someone else's, president-elect's, editor in chief's, son-in-law's**. In the case of those compounds that form their plural by adding **s** to the first word, form the plural possessive case by adding **'s** to the end of the unit: **editors in chief's, sons-in-law's**.

(f) Normally the **'s** or **s'** is reserved for the possessive case of nouns naming animate creatures (human beings and animals). The **of** phrase is commonly used for the possessive case of inanimate nouns: not **the house's roof** but **the roof of the house**. Usage, however, now sanctions the use of **'s** with some inanimate nouns: **a day's wages, a week's work, the year's death toll, the school's policies, the car's performance, the radio's tone**.

21 Possessive Pronoun *its*

Its is the possessive case of the pronoun it; it's is the contraction of it is or it has.

More mistakes have been made with the pronoun **it** than with any other single word in the English language. The mistakes result from confusion about the two **s** forms of this pronoun. **It's** is often used where **its** is the correct form (**The dog broke it's leg** instead of the correct form, **The dog broke its leg**), and **its** is often used where **it's** is the correct form (**Its a shame that the girl broke her leg** instead of the correct form, **It's a shame that the girl broke her leg**).

If you use **it's** for the possessive case of **it**, you are probably influenced by the **'s** that is used to form the possessive case of the singular noun (e.g. **the man's hat**). You might be helped to avoid this mistake if you keep in mind that *none of the personal pronouns uses 's to form its possessive case:* **I/my**, **you/your**, **he/his**, **she/her**, **it/its**, **we/our**, **they/their**. So you should write, **The company lost its lease**.

You might also be helped to avoid this mistake if you remember that the apostrophe has another function in written English: to indicate the omission of one or more letters in an English word, as in contractions (**I'll**, **don't**, **she'd**). The apostrophe in the word **it's** signals the contraction of the expression **it is** or **it has**. So you should write, **It's the first loss that the company has suffered** or **It's come to my attention that you are frequently late**.

Don't let this little word defeat you. Get **it** right, once and for all.

22 Subject/Verb Agreement

The predicate verb should agree in number with its subject.

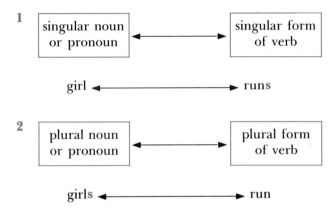

1

| singular noun or pronoun | ◄——————► | singular form of verb |

girl ◄——————► runs

2

| plural noun or pronoun | ◄——————► | plural form of verb |

girls ◄——————► run

22

Some typical examples of faulty agreement:

1. He **don't wear** a hat even in zero weather.

rewrite:

　He **doesn't wear** a hat even in zero weather.

2. The instructor's lack of teaching skills **hinder** the student's learning.

rewrite:

　The instructor's lack of teaching skills **hinders** the student's learning.

3. I hope you will find that my training and experience **fits** the opening that you advertised in the newspaper.

rewrite:

　I hope you will find that my training and experience **fit** the opening that you advertised in the newspaper.

4. The jury **has reached** their decision.

rewrite:

The jury **have reached** their decision.

5. You can easily avoid most of the headaches that **comes** from dealing with the Division of Traffic and Parking.

rewrite:

You can easily avoid most of the headaches that **come** from dealing with the Division of Traffic and Parking.

6. If any one of these directions **are** unclear, you are likely to end up in the wrong place.

rewrite:

If any one of these directions **is** unclear, you are likely to end up in the wrong place.

Expressions like **He don't wear a hat even in zero weather** are not so much "mistakes" in agreement as carry-overs from the dialect that people speak, quite acceptably, in their own communities. Writers should be aware of the standard form of the verb in written prose: **He doesn't wear a hat even in zero weather** (a singular verb with a singular subject).

Most errors of agreement in written prose are the result of carelessness, inadvertence, or uncertainty. The writer often knows better but merely slips up. Errors in agreement often occur when several words intervene between the simple subject of the sentence and the predicate verb, as in sentence **2**: **The instructor's lack of teaching skills hinder the students' learning**. The simple subject of that sentence is **lack**, but because the plural noun **skills** (the object of the preposition **of**) intervened between that singular subject and the verb, the writer was influenced to use the plural form of the verb (**hinder**) instead of the correct singular form (**hinders**). Careful proofreading will often catch such inadvertent errors of agreement.

Errors due to uncertainty are another matter. Uncertainty about whether the verb should be singular or plural arises in cases where (1) the subject is compound, (2) the subject is a collective noun, (3) the subject follows the structure **there is/there are**, and (4) the subject takes the form of a special structure, such as **one of those who** or **this man as well as**. Here are some guidelines for these puzzling cases:

22

(a) Compound subject

(1) Singular subjects joined by **and** usually take a plural verb.

John and his sister **were questioned** by the police.

I hope you will find that my training and experience **fit** the opening that you advertised in the newspaper.

(2) Singular subjects joined by **or** or by the correlative conjunctions **either . . . or**, **neither . . . nor** take a singular verb.

John or his sister **runs** the store during the week.

Neither the nurse nor Dr. Bruce **is worried** about the patient's condition.

(3) When both subjects are plural, the verb is plural.

The detectives and the insurance agents **have expressed** their belief in the innocence of the brother and sister.

Neither the detectives nor the insurance agents **have expressed** any doubts about the innocence of the brother and sister.

(4) When one subject is singular and the other subject is plural and the subjects are joined by **or** or by the correlative conjunctions **either . . . or**, **neither . . . nor**, the verb agrees in number with the closer subject.

Either John or his parents **work** in the store on Sunday.

Neither the brothers nor the sister **appears** to be cooperative.

However, plural or singular subjects joined by the correlative conjunctions **both . . . and** or **not only . . . but (also)** take a plural verb.

Both John and his sister **have agreed** to cooperate with the police.

Not only the brother but also the sister **appear** to be cooperative.

(b) Collective noun as subject

(1) If the collective noun is considered as a *group*, the verb is singular.

The jury **has made up** its mind.

The committee **was elected** unanimously.

The number of students who failed **has increased** by 50 percent.

(2) If the collective noun is considered as *individuals*, each acting on his or her own, the verb is plural.

The jury **have made** up their minds.

The committee **wish** to offer their congratulations to the new chairperson.

A number of students **have asked** the dean for an extension.

(c) The structure **there is/there are**, **there was/there were**

(1) If the delayed or real subject following **there** is singular, the verb is singular.

There **is** a remarkable consensus among the committee members.

(2) If the delayed or real subject following **there** is plural, the verb is plural.

There **were** ten dissenting votes among the stockholders.

(d) Special structures

(1) In the structure **one of the** [plural nouns—e.g. *women*] **who**, the predicate verb of the **who** clause is plural, because the antecedent of the subject **who** is the plural noun rather than the singular one.

Sylvester is one of the men who **refuse** to accept the ruling. (*here the antecedent of **who** is the plural noun **men***)

(2) Exception: if **the only** precedes **one of the** [plural noun—e.g. **men**] **who**, the predicate verb of the **who** clause is singular, because the subject of **who** in that case refers to the singular **one** rather than to the plural object of the preposition **of**.

Sylvester is the only one of the men who **refuses** to accept the ruling.

If any one of these directions **is** unclear, you are likely to end up in the wrong place.

(3) A singular subject followed by structures such as **as well as**, **in addition to**, **together with** takes a singular verb.

(Of course, a plural subject followed by any of these structures would take a plural verb. See the third example below.)

The sergeant, as well as his superior officer, **praises** his platoon.

Diane Leonard, along with her roommate, **has denied** the charges.

The students, together with their counselor, **deny** that there has been any distribution of drugs in the dorms.

(4) Nouns that do not end in **s** but that are plural in meaning take a plural verb.

The bacteria **require** constant attention.

These data **are** consistent with the judge's findings.

The deer **are running** loose in the state park.

(5) Nouns that end in **s** but that are singular in meaning take a singular verb.

My grandmother's scissors **was** very dull.

Ten dollars **is** a fair price for the coat.

Two weeks **seems** a long time when you are waiting for someone you love.

(6) Noun clauses serving as the subject of the sentence always take a singular verb.

That Linda decided to go on a diet **pleases** me very much.

What caused all the trouble **was** the animosity between the two factions.

(7) In inverted structures, where the subject follows the verb, a singular subject takes a singular verb, and a plural subject takes a plural verb.

At each checkpoint **stands** a heavily armed soldier.

Happy **were** they to see us arrive.

Among the crew **were** Carson, Barrows, and Fairchild.

23 Noun/Pronoun Agreement

A pronoun must agree in person, number, and gender with its antecedent noun.

Examples of faulty agreement between a pronoun and its antecedent:

1. Even early in the morning, **no one** should expect to get a parking space close to the building where **they** work.

rewrite:

Even early in the morning, **no one** should expect to get a parking space close to the building where **he or she** works.

2. **Each student** was allowed to voice **his** opinion on the issue being discussed.

rewrite:
   All students were allowed to voice **their** opinions on the issue being discussed.

3. Many words in our language can claim television as **its** birthplace.

rewrite:
   Many words in our language can claim television as **their** birthplace.

23

4. A **family** cannot go camping these days without a truckload of gadgets to make **your** campsite look like home.

rewrite:
   A **family** cannot go camping these days without a truckload of gadgets to make **their** campsite look like home.

Pronouns, which are substitutes for nouns, share the following features with nouns: **number** (singular or plural) and **gender** (masculine or feminine or neuter). What nouns and pronouns do not share is the full range of **person**. All nouns are **third person** exclusively; but some pronouns are **first person** (**I, we**), some are **second person** (**you**), and some are **third person** (**he, she, it, they, one, some, none, all, everybody**).

A firm grammatical principle is that a pronoun must correspond with whatever features of person, number, and gender it has in common with its antecedent noun. A second-person pronoun (*you*) should not be linked with a third-person noun (*family*) (see sentence **4**).

Sentences **1** and **2** exhibit the problem we have with noun-pronoun agreement because the English language has no convenient pronoun for indicating masculine-or-feminine gender. It has been a common practice in the past to use the generic **he** (**him, his**) to refer to nouns of common gender like **student**, **teacher**, **writer**, **candidate**,

driver. In recent years, however, the use of generic **he** and its derivative forms (**his**, **him**) to refer to singular nouns that could be either masculine or feminine has been considered an example of the sexist bias of the English language. Many writers today are making a genuine effort to avoid offending readers with any kind of sexist language.

How do you deal with the agreement problem exemplified in sentence 1? The subject of that sentence is *one*, the closest thing that the English language has to a pronoun that can refer to either a masculine or a feminine person. But what singular pronoun can you use to refer to the common-gender pronoun *one*? One solution is to use the phrase **he or she**, as we have done in rewriting sentence 1: "Even early in the morning, no **one** should expect to get a parking space close to the building where **he or she** works." Another solution that is sometimes available is to turn the common-gender noun into a plural, as we have done in revising sentence 2. Instead of using **each student** as the subject of the sentence, we change the subject to the plural form, **all students**, and then we can use the plural pronoun **their** to refer to **students**: "All **students** were allowed to voice **their** opinions on the issue being discussed."

Mismatchings of nouns and pronouns in person and gender are not very common in written prose. Most mismatchings of nouns and pronouns involve number—a singular pronoun referring to a plural noun (**words . . . it**, as in sentence 3) or a plural pronoun referring to a singular noun (e.g., using **them** to refer to **soldier**). Another agreement problem derives from the ambiguity of number of such pronouns as **everyone**, **everybody**, **all**, **none**, **some**, **each**. Although there are exceptions, the following guidelines are generally reliable:

(a) **Everyone**, **everybody**, **anybody**, **anyone** invariably take singular verbs and, in formal usage at least, should be referred to by a singular pronoun.

> **Everyone** brings **his or her** schedule cards to the bursar's office.
>
> **Anybody** who wants to run in the race has to pay **her** entry fee by Friday.

(b) **All** and **some** are singular or plural according to the context. If the **of** phrase following the pronoun specifies a *mass* or a *bulk* of something, the pronoun is singular. If the **of** phrase specifies a *number* of things or persons, the pronoun is plural.

> **Some** of the fabric has lost **its** coloring.
>
> **All** of the sugar was spoiled by **its** own chemical imbalance.
>
> **Some** of the students complained about **their** dormitory rooms.
>
> **All** of the women registered **their** protests at City Hall.

(c) **None** is singular or plural according to the context. (The distinction in particular cases is sometimes so subtle that a writer could justify either a singular or a plural pronoun.)

> **None** of the young men **was** willing to turn in **his** driver's license. (*But* **were . . . their** *could also be justified in this case.*)
>
> **None** of the young men **were** as tall as **their** fathers. (*Here it would be harder to justify the singular forms* **was . . . his**.)

(d) **Each** is singular.

> **Each** of the mothers declared **her** undying allegiance to democracy.

(e) For guidelines about the number of collective nouns (like *family*, *team*), see **(b)** in the previous section (22).

If you match up your pronouns in person, number, and

23

gender with their antecedent nouns, you will make it easier for your reader to figure out what the pronouns refer to.

24 Pronoun Antecedent

A pronoun should have a clear antecedent.

Examples of no antecedent or an unclear antecedent for the pronoun (an antecedent is a noun in a previous group of words to which a pronoun can refer):

1. The Acme Corporation has taken the safety program too lightly. In fact, it has taken it so lightly that **it** has cost the company over $7 million in insurance claims.

rewrite:

   The Acme Corporation has taken the safety program too lightly. In fact, it has taken the program so lightly that this indifference has cost the company over $7 million in insurance claims.

2. Note that this area on the monitor screen is quite near the menu of this software program, **which** is intentional.

rewrite:

   Note that this area on the monitor screen is quite near the menu of this software program, a placement that is intentional.

3. Marilyn told her mother that **her** purse was on the dresser.

rewrite:

   Marilyn told her mother, "Your purse is on the dresser."

   or

   Marilyn told her mother, "My purse is on the dresser."

4. The team's decision was to cancel all doubleheaders on the schedule, but **it** could not get the approval of the other teams in the league.

rewrite:

The team decided to cancel all doubleheaders on the schedule, but it could not get the approval of the other teams in the league.

5. The definition of *dude* is remarkably similar to the definition for *dandy* and *fop*. **This** raises the question of whether the word *dude* really has a meaning distinctive from that of the other two words.

rewrite:

The definition of *dude* is remarkably similar to the definition for *dandy* and *fop*. This similarity raises the question of whether the word *dude* really has a meaning distinctive from that of the other two words.

24

Careless handling of the pronoun often blocks communication between writer and reader. As the writer, you usually know what you meant the pronoun to stand for, but if there is no antecedent (a noun in the previous group of words to which the pronoun can refer) or if it is difficult to find the noun to which the pronoun refers, your reader will not know—and will have to guess—what the pronoun stands for.

Whenever you use a pronoun, check to see whether there is a noun in the previous group of words that could be put in the place of the pronoun. Let us apply this test to sentence **1**. The pronoun **it** occurs three times in that sentence. When you try to find the noun in the previous group of words to which each **it** refers, you discover that each **it** has a different antecedent. The first **it** seems to refer to **Acme Corporation**. The second **it** seems to refer to **safety program**. But what does the third **it** refer to? You should avoid using the same pronoun in a sentence when each one refers to a different antecedent. Note how we rewrote the two sentences to remove the unclear references: **The Acme Corporation has taken the safety program too lightly. In fact, it has taken the program so lightly that this indifference has cost the company over $7 million in insurance claims.** Now the reader should have no difficulty figuring out what the two sentences are saying.

Sentence **3** is another example of an unclear antecedent. The pronoun reference is unclear because the pronoun **her** is ambiguous—that is, there are two nouns to which the feminine, singular pronoun **her** could refer: **Marilyn** and **mother**. So we cannot tell whether it was the mother's purse or Marilyn's purse that was on the dresser. If the context in which that sentence occurred doesn't help us determine whose purse was being referred to, one way to remove the amibiguity is to turn the sentence into a direct quotation, as we did in the revision.

Although the use of the pronoun **this** or **that** to refer to a whole idea in a previous clause or sentence has long been a common practice in spoken English, you should be aware that by using the demonstrative pronoun **this** or **that** in that way, you run the risk that the reference of the pronoun will be vague or ambiguous for your readers. If you do not want to run that risk, you can use **this** or **that** (or the corresponding plural, **these** or **those**) as an adjective instead of as a pronoun. The adjective would go before some noun summing up what **this** or **that** stands for. In sentence **5**, we can avoid the vague pronoun reference by using the phrase **this similarity** instead of the pronoun **this**.

The use of the relative pronoun **which** or **that** to refer to a whole idea in the main clause rather than to a specific noun in that clause is also becoming more common. But there is a risk in this use similar to the one that attends the use of **this** or **that** to refer to a whole idea. We can save the reader from being even momentarily baffled by the **which** in sentence **2** by supplying a summary noun to serve as the antecedent for that relative pronoun. In revising sentence **2**, we have inserted **placement** as the antecedent for the relative pronoun **that**.

The problem with the pronoun reference in sentence **4** stems from the linguistic fact that a pronoun does not readily reveal its antecedent if it refers to a noun that is functioning in a subordinate structure such as a possessive (the **school's** principal), a modifier of a noun (the **school** term), or an object of a preposition (in the **school**). One remedy for the vague pronoun reference in sentence **4** is to use the noun **team** in the second clause rather than the pronoun **it** (". . . but the **team** could not get the approval of the other teams in the league"). Another remedy is the one we used in rewriting sentence **4**: making **team** the subject of the first clause so that the **it** in the second clause would have a clear antecedent.

25 Dangling Modifier

An introductory verbal or verbal phrase must find its "doer" in the subject of the main clause.

Examples of "dangling" verbal phrases:

1. Revolving at a rate of 2200 revolutions per minute, the janitor turned off the overheated generator.

rewrite:

Revolving at a rate of 2200 revolutions per minute, the overheated generator was turned off by the janitor.

or

The janitor turned off the overheated generator, which was revolving at a rate of 2200 revolutions per minute.

2. After finding a good advisor, your next challenge will be to make an appointment with that person at a convenient time.

rewrite:

After finding a good advisor, you should then make an appointment with that person at a convenient time.

3. To facilitate this operation, measurements will be taken of the distance that the throw-arm travels whenever a box is discharged from the assembly line.

rewrite:

To facilitate this operation, the engineers will measure the distance that the throw-arm travels whenever a box is discharged from the assembly line.

4. In order to achieve a quick response from the pneumatic jack, it was necessary to install a sturdy air-pressure tank.

rewrite:

In order to achieve a quick response from the pneumatic jack, you must install a sturdy air-pressure tank.

In English, an introductory verbal phrase (dominated by a participle, a gerund, or an infinitive) naturally adheres to the subject of the main clause. When the subject of the main clause is *not* the "doer" of the action indicated in the verbal, we say that the verbal **dangles**—that it is not attached to the proper agent. In each of the sample sentences, the subject of the main clause is not the "doer" of the action specified by the introductory verbal (**revolving**, **finding**, **to facilitate**, **to achieve**). In sentence **4**, both infinitives (**to achieve**, **to install**) are left dangling: there is nobody doing the achieving or the installing.

Sometimes in revising the sentence to make the subject of the main clause the doer of the action specified in our introductory verbal, we have to resort to a rather awkward passive verb, as we did in revising sentence **1**. If we start a sentence with a verbal phrase, we cannot start the main clause of that sentence with a structure like **there is** or **it is** (see sentence **4**).

To prevent dangling verbals, writers should always make sure that the subject of the main clause is the doer of the action specified in the preceding verbal.

26 Misplaced Modifier

Misplaced modifiers lead to a misreading of the sentence.

Examples of misplaced modifiers:

1. The plan that they formulated **quickly** forced them to assume a strong position.

rewrite:

   The plan that they quickly formulated forced them to assume a strong position.

                              or

   The plan that they formulated forced them quickly to assume a strong position.

2. In the School of Architecture, students are **only** permitted to enter the program in the fall of the year.

rewrite:
> In the School of Architecture, students are permitted to enter the program only in the fall of the year.

3. I had already thought about how the roller could be adapted **at the outset of the project**.

rewrite:
> At the outset of the project, I had already thought about how the roller could be adapted.

4. Emil **even** limps when nobody is watching him.

rewrite:
> Emil limps even when nobody is watching him.

5. She paid $180 for a dress at the **local boutique** that she despised.

rewrite:
> At the local boutique, she paid $180 for a dress that she despised.

Because English is a language that depends heavily on word order to protect meaning, related words, phrases, and clauses should be placed as close as possible to one another. Adverbial and adjectival modifiers especially must be placed as close as possible to words that they modify. Failure to juxtapose related words, phrases, or clauses may lead to a misreading—that is, to a reading different from what the author intended.

In sentence **1**, we have an example of what is called a **squinting modifier**, a modifier that looks in two directions at once. In that sentence, the adverb **quickly** sits between two verbs that it could modify—**formulated** and **forced**. If the writer intends the adverb to modify the act of *formulating* rather than the act of *forcing*, the position of **quickly** should be shifted so that the sentence reads as follows: **The plan that they quickly formulated forced them to assume a strong position.** If, however, the writer intends the adverb to modify the act of forcing, **quickly** should be shifted to a position between **them** and **to assume**.

Because the adverb **only** in sentence **2** is placed before the verb **permitted**, it is modifying a word that the author did not intend it to modify. **Only** should be shifted to a position before the phrase that the author meant it to modify: **only in the fall of the year**.

Because the prepositional phrase **at the outset of the project** has been put in the wrong place in sentence **3**, it does not modify the verb phrase that it should be modifying (**had thought**) and therefore does not say what the writer intended to say. Note that in the revision of sentence **3**, the prepositional phrase has been shifted to the beginning of the sentence so that it will modify what it should be modifying.

Chances are that the writer of sentence **4** did not intend **even** to modify the act of *limping*. Shifting **even** will make the sentence say what the writer probably meant to say: **Emil limps even when nobody is watching him**.

In sentence **5**, shifting the position of the phrase **at the local boutique** and the position of the clause **that she despised** makes the sentence say what the author undoubtedly meant it to say.

Reading sentences aloud will sometimes reveal the misplacement of modifying words, phrases, and clauses.

26

27 Parallelism

Preserve parallel structure by using units of the same grammatical kind.

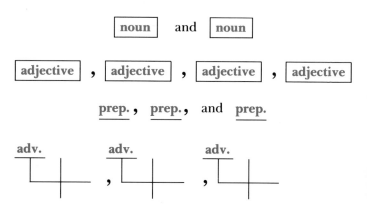

Examples of breakdown in parallelism:

1. I am now disposed **to redesign** the operation of your department or **to changing** the position of the equipment and the offices.
   (*infinitive phrase, gerund phrase*)

rewrite:

   I am now disposed **to redesign** the operation of your department or **to change** the position of the equipment and the offices.

2. I also wished to find out how far a writer could go to get the precise word for the context, even if the word was not **traditional usage** or **grammatically correct**.
   (*noun, adjective*)

rewrite:

   I also wished to find out how far a writer could go to get the

precise word for the context, even if the word did not conform
to **traditional usage** or to **correct grammar**.

3. First of all, Inez was an **adult, married,** and **had a young
   daughter**.
   (*noun, adjective, verb phrase*)

rewrite:

First of all, Inez was an **adult**, a **married woman**, and the
mother of a young daughter.

4. The campus police spend a good part of their day **looking** for
   cars parked in the wrong place, **checking** parking stickers, and
   arrange to have illegally parked cars towed away.
   (*participle, participle, verb*)

rewrite:

The campus police spend a good part of their day **looking** for
cars parked in the wrong place, **checking** parking stickers, and
arranging to have illegally parked cars towed away.

5. **Your company** and **what its potential is** are of great interest to
   me.
   (*noun, noun clause*)

rewrite:

Your company and **its potential** are of great interest to me.

6. As an industrial engineer, I am trained to analyze and improve
   work methods, **both from** an "efficiency" point of view **and** a
   "worker comfort" point of view.
   (*violation of parallelism with correlative conjunctions*)

rewrite:

As an industrial engineer, I am trained to analyze and improve
work methods, **both from** an "efficiency" point of view **and
from** a "worker comfort" point of view.

7. They **not only** persuade the family that they must plan a
   sensible budget **but also** that a sensible budget will enable them
   to buy more of the necessities of life.
   (*violation of parallelism with correlative conjunctions*)

rewrite:

> They persuade the family not only **that they must plan a sensible budget** but also **that a sensible budget will enable them to buy more of the necessities of life**.

The principle governing parallel structure is that a pair or a series (three or more) of units serving the same function in a sentence should be composed of similar elements—e.g., nouns with nouns, adjectives with adjectives, not a mixture of nouns and adjectives. A breakdown in parallelism wrenches coherence because it disrupts the expectation that when a series starts out with one kind of element, it will stay with that element.

The obvious way to correct a breakdown in parallelism is to convert all the members of the pair or the series to units of the same structure or part of speech. In converting all the members of a pair or a series to units of the same structure or part of speech, we sometimes have an either/or option available, but usually one of the options will be stylistically preferable to the other. In revising sentence **1**, for instance, we could elect the option of using a pair of gerunds instead of a pair of infinitives. If we did, the revision would take this form:

> I am now disposed **to redesigning** the operation of your department or **to changing** the position of the equipment and the offices.

The other sample sentences, however, do not readily lend themselves to alternative revisions. In revising sentence **3**, for instance, we could convert the first two items in the series into adjectives, so that the sentence would read, "First of all, Inez was **adult**, **married**, and. . . ." But we cannot follow through with that part of speech because there is no adjective form of the third element in the series, **had a young daughter**. Our only option in revising sentence **3** is to convert all three items in the series to noun phrases.

Sentences **6** and **7** illustrate a violation of parallelism when correlative conjunctions are used: **either . . . or, neither . . . nor, both . . . and, not (only) . . . but (also)**. The principle operating with correlative conjunctions is that the same grammatical structure must be on the right-hand side of both conjunctions. We can more easily see the breakdown in parallelism if we lay out sentence **7** in two layers:

27

> They **not only** persuade the family that they must plan a sensible budget
>> **but also** that a sensible budget will enable them to buy more of the necessities of life.

On the right-hand side of **not only**, there is this grammatical sequence: a verb (**persuade**), a noun (**the family**), and a noun clause (**that they must plan a sensible budget**). But on the right-hand side of **but also**, there is only a noun clause (**that a sensible budget will enable them to buy more of the necessities of life**). The faulty parallelism can be revised in either of two ways:

> They **not only** persuade the family that they must plan a sensible budget
>> **but also** persuade the family that a sensible budget will enable them to buy more of the necessities of life.
>
> **or**
>
> They persuade the family **not only** that they must plan a sensible budget
>> **but also** that a sensible budget will enable them to buy more of the necessities of life.

In both revisions, we now have the same grammatical structure on the right-hand side of both correlative conjunctions. But because the second revision has fewer words and less repetition than the first one, it is probably the better of the two revisions stylistically.

Note how parallelism is preserved in the following two sentences using correlative conjunctions:

> **Either** he will love the one and hate the other, **or** he will hate the one and love the other.

> He will **either** love the one and hate the other **or** hate the one and love the other.

The principle governing parallelism: **like must be joined with like**.

28 Subordinate Conjunction *that*

Use the subordinate conjunction *that* if it will prevent a possible misreading.

Examples where it would be advisable to insert **that**:

1. The first thing done was ∧ the frame of the extension was welded onto the old frame.

rewrite:

> The first thing done was **that** the frame of the extension was welded onto the old frame.

2. My father believed ∧ his doctor, who was a boyhood friend, was wholly trustworthy.

rewrite:

> My father believed **that** his doctor, who was a boyhood friend, was wholly trustworthy.

3. Keep in mind ∧ this university has many opportunities to offer.

rewrite:

> Keep in mind **that** this university has many opportunities to offer.

4. Students need to make sure not only that they promptly apply for financial aid but ∧ the aid arrives in time for them to pay their fees.

rewrite:

Students need to make sure not only that they promptly apply for financial aid but **that** the aid arrives in time for them to pay their fees.

5. The police reported ∧ as soon as they found out that the car was stolen they sent out a description of it to all squad cars on duty.

rewrite:

The police reported **that** as soon as they found out that the car was stolen they sent out a description of it to all squad cars on duty.

28

The tendency of our language is toward economy of means. So we omit syllables in such contractions as **he's, she'll, we'd, won't**, and we resort to such common elliptical expressions as **not all [of] the men; she is taller than I [am tall]; when [I was] in the fourth grade, I went to the zoo with my mother**. We also frequently omit the conjunction **that**, which introduces a noun clause serving as the object of a verb, as in "He said [**that**] he was going" and "He announced [**that**] I was a candidate for office."

Whether to use the conjunction **that** in written prose will be a problem only when a noun clause is being used as the direct object of a verb—but not in every instance of such use. If there is no chance that a sentence will be misread, it is all right, even in written prose, to omit **that**. But if there is a chance that a noun phrase following the verb may be read as the object of the verb rather than as the subject of the subsequent clause, then we can prevent even a momentary misreading by inserting **that** at the beginning of the noun clause. What follows may make all of this discussion clearer.

In a sentence such as "He believed they were going," it is safe to omit **that** after **believed** because **they** cannot possibly be read as the object of **believed**. (If **they** were the object of the verb here, the pronoun would have to be **them**—**He believed them**.) But in a sentence like **2**, it is not only possible but likely that the noun phrase **his doctor** will initially be read as the object of **believed** (**he believed his doctor**). Of course, as soon as we come to the predicate **was wholly trustworthy**, we realize that we have misread the sentence, and so we have to back up and reread the sentence as the writer intended it to be read. But the writer could have prevented that initial misreading by inserting **that** after **believed**—**My father believed that his doctor, who was a boyhood friend, was wholly trustworthy.** Then the sentence can be read in only one way—the way in which the writer intended it to be read.

Read the other sample sentences aloud, the first time omitting **that**, the second time inserting **that** where the (∧) is. By doing this double reading of the sentences aloud, you will notice how the insertion of **that** ensures that the sentences will be read in the way the writer intended them to be read.

When a reader has to reread a sentence in order to make sense of it, the writer is often the one to blame. Inserting **that** where it is necessary or advisable is one way to spare readers from having to reread a sentence.

29 Sentence Fragment

Avoid the careless or indefensible use of sentence fragments.

——————— •

Examples of questionable sentence fragments:

1. They acquire not only a degree but an education. **An education that will be invaluable to them for life.**

rewrite:

They acquire not only a degree but an education, an education that will be invaluable to them for life.

2. **The reason for Holden's disappointment being that his sister wasn't there to comfort him.**

rewrite:

The reason for Holden's disappointment was that his sister wasn't there to comfort him.

3. Before enrolling for an elective course, students should gather as much information as they can. **The professor's grading policy, the number of papers he assigns during the semester, the kinds of examination he gives, and his attendance policy.**

rewrite:

Before enrolling for an elective course, students should gather as much information as they can: the professor's grading policy, the number of papers he assigns during the semester, the kinds of examination he gives, and his attendance policy.

4. They tried to console the mother for the tragic death of her son. **Although they soon realized that no words they could utter would comfort her.**

rewrite:

They tried to console the mother for the tragic death of her son, although they soon realized that no words they could utter would comfort her.

A sentence fragment can be defined as a string of words, appearing between an initial capital letter and a final period or question mark, that does one of the following: lacks a subject or a finite-verb predicate (or both); has a subject and a finite-verb predicate but is made part of a larger structure by a relative pronoun (**who**, **which**, **that**) or by a subordinating conjunction (**although**, **because**, **if**, **when**, and so on). According to that definition, all four of the sample sentences above qualify as sentence fragments.

In sentence **4**, for instance, the string of words beginning with **although** and terminating with a period is a sentence fragment because, even though it has a subject (**they**) and a finite-verb predicate (**realized**), it is turned into a dependent clause by the subordinating conjunction **although**. If, instead of using the subordinating conjunction **although**, the writer had used a coordinating conjunction (**but**) or a conjunctive adverb (**however**) in the initial position of that clause, that string of words would be a complete sentence. If **although** is used to begin that string of words, however, that string must be made part of the preceding independent clause.

The string of words in example **2** and the second string of words in example **1** are sentence fragments because they both lack a finite-verb predicate. The second string of words in **1** has a finite-verb predicate (**will be**), but that verb is the predicate of the dependent adjective clause beginning with **that**. The second example has a verbal in it (**being**), but that participle by itself cannot constitute the predicate of an independent clause. Note that we made this string of words a complete sentence simply by substituting the finite verb **was** for the participle **being**.

The second string of words in example **3** has two finite verbs in it (**assigns** and **gives**), but both of those verbs serve as the predicate of dependent adjective clauses (**papers**

[that] he assigns, **kinds of examination [that] he gives**).
Note that we have joined that predicateless string of words
to the previous independent clause by replacing the period
with a colon and by reducing the capital letter in **The** to a
lowercase **t**. As a result of the revision, the two strings of
words stand as a single complete sentence.

Whether a string of words constitutes a complete sentence or only a sentence fragment is a grammatical concern; whether the use of a sentence fragment is appropriate in a particular context is a rhetorical or stylistic concern.
It is a fact of life that we sometimes communicate with one
another in sentence fragments. Note for instance the following exchange:

> Where are you going tonight?
> The movies.
> Who with?
> Jack.
> Where?
> The Palace.
> What time?
> About 8:30.
> By car?
> No, by bus.
> Can I go?
> Sure.

Once the context of that dialogue was established, both
speakers communicated in fragmentary sentences. Notice,
however, that the dialogue had to be initiated by a complete sentence (the question **Where are you going to-
night?**) and that later the first speaker had to resort again
to a complete sentence (**Can I go?**) because there was no
way to phrase that question clearly in a fragmentary way.

Native speakers of a language can converse in fragments because each of them is capable of mentally supplying what is missing from an utterance. When in response to the initial question the second speaker answers, **The movies**, that phrase conveys a meaning because the first speaker is able to supply, mentally, the missing elements in the fragmentary reply: **[I am going to] the movies.**

29

All of us have encountered sentence fragments in the written prose of some very reputable writers. Predicateless sentences are most likely to be found in mood-setting descriptive and narrative prose, as in this first paragraph of Charles Dickens's novel *Bleak House*:

> London, Michaelmas Term lately over, and the Lord Chancellor sitting in Lincoln's Inn Hall. Implacable November weather. As much mud in the streets, as if the waters had but newly retired from the face of the earth, and it would not be wonderful to meet a Megalosaurus, forty feet long or so, waddling like an elephantine lizard up Holborn Hill. Smoke lowering down from chimney-pots, making a soft black drizzle, with flakes of soot in it as big as full-grown snow-flakes—gone into mourning, one might imagine, for the death of the sun. Dogs, undistinguishable in mire. Horses, scarcely better; splashed to their blinkers. Foot passengers, jostling one another's umbrellas, in a general infection of ill-temper, and losing their foothold at street-corners, where tens of thousands of other foot passengers have been slipping and sliding since the day broke (if this day ever broke), adding new deposits to the crust upon crust of mud, sticking at those points tenaciously to the pavement and accumulating at compound interest.

In that paragraph, there are a few clauses (that is, groups of words with a subject and a finite-verb predicate), but the paragraph consists primarily of nouns and noun phrases, some of them modified by participial phrases (e.g., **sitting in Lincoln's Inn Hall**, **splashed to their blinkers**, **jostling**

one another's umbrellas). (It might be a good exercise for you to go through the paragraph and see if you can distinguish the sentence fragments from the complete sentences.) Although the passage is largely lacking in statements made with finite verbs, the sequence of fragmentary sentences does create effects that Dickens could not have achieved—or achieved as well—with complete sentences.

The points to be made in citing these examples of spoken and written discourse are (1) that sentence fragments are a part of the English language (in that sense, they are "grammatical"), (2) that in certain contexts they do communicate meaning, and (3) that in some circumstances and for some purposes they are appropriate and therefore acceptable, effective, and even stylistically desirable. But you should be aware of what you are doing. You should be aware that you are deliberately using a sentence fragment instead of a complete sentence; otherwise, you will be guilty of a *careless* use of a sentence fragment. And you should have some purpose or effect in mind when you use a sentence fragment; otherwise, you will be guilty of an *indefensible* use of a sentence fragment. In every case, you should be aware of the possibility that the sentence fragment may not communicate clearly with your readers.

30 Comma Splice

Independent clauses cannot be spliced simply with a comma.

Examples of comma splices:

1. We do not have to infer the author's purpose, it is spelled out quite clearly for us.

rewrite:

   We do not have to infer the author's purpose; it is spelled out quite clearly for us.

2. As for the material we will use, steel is relatively inexpensive, however it is very heavy.

rewrite:

   As for the material we will use, steel is relatively inexpensive, but it is very heavy.

3. It was not worth my while to argue with her, I just ignored her and went away.

rewrite:

   Because it was not worth my while to argue with her, I just ignored her and went away.

4. Don't let them get away with that kind of nonsense, stand up for your rights.

rewrite:

   Don't let them get away with that kind of nonsense. Stand up for your rights.

A comma splice is the result of joining independent clauses with nothing but a comma. *A comma is a separating device, not a joining device.* A comma splice is, therefore, an error in punctuation, but since punctuation is, for the written language, the grammatical equivalent of vocal intonation in the spoken language, this error in punctuation can also be considered an error in grammar.

Independent clauses must be joined either by a coordinating conjunction (**and**, **but**, **or**, **for**, **nor**, **yet**, **so**) or by a semicolon. In addition to these two ways of properly splicing independent clauses, there are two other ways of fixing up a comma splice: by making separate sentences of the two clauses and by subordinating one of the clauses. Using these four methods in turn, let us correct the comma splice in the first sample sentence above.

(a) Insert the appropriate coordinating conjunction after the comma:

> We do not have to infer the author's purpose, **for** it is spelled out quite clearly for us.

30

(b) Substitute a semicolon for the comma:

> We do not have to infer the author's purpose; it is spelled out quite clearly for us.

(c) Put a period at the end of the first independent clause and begin a new sentence with the first word of the second independent clause:

> We do not have to infer the author's purpose. It is spelled out quite clearly for us.

(d) Subordinate one of the independent clauses:

> We do not have to infer the author's purpose, **because** it is spelled out quite clearly for us.

Although these four ways of repairing a comma splice are always available, one of them will usually be better in a particular instance. In sentence **1**, splicing the two clauses with a semicolon would probably be the best way, because the semicolon between the two independent clauses effects the closest union of the two related clauses and allows the reader to infer that the second clause provides a reason for what was said in the first clause. We have made our choice of the semicolon on stylistic grounds; grammatically, the other three options are equally correct.

See **66** and **67** in the section on punctuation for the proper use of the semicolon.

31 Fused Sentence or Run-on Sentence

Do not run independent clauses together without a conjunction or the proper punctuation.

Examples of independent clauses run together:

1. Why am I qualified to speak on this subject I just finished three dreadful years of high school.

rewrite:

   Why am I qualified to speak on this subject? I just finished three dreadful years of high school.

2. Nobody in the stands could tell which horse had won the race in fact even the officials could not tell after looking at the photographs of the finish.

rewrite:

   Nobody in the stands could tell which horse had won the race. In fact, even the officials could not tell after looking at the photographs of the finish.

3. There are some commuters who don't even bother to park on campus instead they park in streets east of the university.

rewrite:

   There are some commuters who don't even bother to park on campus; instead they park in streets east of the university.

4. My piano lessons were not very beneficial for me I was always too tired to practice.

rewrite:

   My piano lessons were not very beneficial for me **because** I was always too tired to practice.

The term commonly used to label two or more independent clauses that have been run together without any conjunction or punctuation is **fused sentence** or **run-on sentence**. Fused sentences are not as common in writing as comma splices; but when they occur, they are even more of a stumbling block for readers than comma splices. If the writers of the sample sentences above had read their strings of words aloud, they would have detected a natural stopping place—a place where the expression of one thought ended and the expression of another began.

31

Once the writers had detected the fused or run-on sentences, they could have then considered how best to revise them. Fused sentences can be corrected in the same four ways that comma splices can be corrected:

(a) Join the independent clauses with the appropriate co-ordinating conjunction (the two clauses in sentence 4 could be joined with the coordinating conjunction **for** instead of with the subordinating conjunction **because**).

(b) Splice the independent clauses with a semicolon (see the revision of sentence 3 above).

(c) Make separate sentences of the independent clauses (see the revisions of sentences 1 and 2 above).

(d) Subordinate one of the independent clauses (see the revision of sentence 4 above).

As with comma splices, all four of these ways are usually available for correcting a fused sentence, but in a particular instance, one of them will probably be better than the others. Furthermore, some fused sentences do not readily lend themselves to correction by any one of the four means. For instance, because sentence 1 fuses a question and a statement—**Why am I qualified to speak on this subject** (question) and **I just finished three dreadful years of high school** (statement), it most readily lends itself to correction by the third method, that of making separate sentences of the two clauses. Sentence 3 does not readily lend itself to correction by the use of a coordinating conjunction. The coordinating conjunctions **or**, **nor**, **for**, **yet**, **so** just do not fit with the sense of the two clauses. Depending on the larger context in which the sentence occurred, joining the two independent clauses with the coordinating conjunction **and** or **but** might work, but this way of revising the sentence would not be as satisfactory as joining the clauses with a semicolon.

A sentence like **All the apples were picked before the first frost but many of them were unfit to eat**, which lacks a comma before the coordinating conjunction **but**, is not to be regarded as a fused sentence. It lacks the comma in compound sentences called for in **60**, but unlike the examples of fused sentences at the beginning of this section, it has a coordinating conjunction (**but**) to join the two independent clauses. Simply putting a comma in front of **but** would correct that sentence.

Reading your prose aloud will usually disclose instances where independent clauses have been run together.

32 Confusing Sentence

Choose words and put them together so that they make sense.

Examples of confusing or puzzling sentences.

1. In these particular cases that I have heard about, result in the person paying for the towing bill and the parking.

rewrite:

In the particular cases that I have heard about, the result is that the offending person pays the towing bill and the parking bill.

2. In addition, I will utilize human factors engineering concepts to produce a man-machine interface that will improve the operation of the assembly line.

rewrite:

In addition, I will utilize human factors and engineering concepts to produce a robot that will improve the operation of the assembly line.

3. The cost of insulating a house in this region is more than repaid in rapidly advancing economy with greater material comforts homewise and for peace of mind.

rewrite:

The cost of insulating a house in this region is more than repaid in rapidly accelerating savings and in the ever-increasing material comforts in the home that can produce peace of mind.

4. These methods are not considered ideal for routine tests because of however you think of them boredom sets in and the patients lose interest in the process.

rewrite:

These methods are not considered ideal for routine tests because, regardless of what you think of the methods, boredom sets in and the patients lose interest in the process.

5. William Faulkner presents in his short story "Barn Burning" a human that is as nonhuman as is feasible to a person's mind.

rewrite:

William Faulkner presents in his short story "Barn Burning" a character that is as unlike a human being as a person could imagine.

A confusing or puzzling sentence is one that because of some flaw in the *choice* of words or in the *arrangement* of words reveals no meaning or a scrambled meaning or a vague meaning. Unlike the stylistic flaws discussed in **40**, **41**, and **42** in the next section on Style—flaws that produce awkward or imprecise or inept sentences—this flaw of diction or arrangement produces what might be called a "non-English" sentence—a sentence that is semantically or grammatically impossible in the English language. For example, a sentence like "The ice cube froze" is a non-English sentence because of the choice of the semantically incompatible words **ice cube** and **froze**. (We can say, "The water froze," but we are uttering nonsense if we say, "The ice cube froze.") A sentence like "Harshly me teacher scolded the yesterday" is a non-English sentence because English grammar does not allow that arrangement of words. To make sense, those words would have to be arranged in an order like "The teacher scolded me harshly yesterday."

Some of the sample sentences above are confusing or puzzling mainly because of the choice of words. In sentence **5**, for instance, there is some incompatibility between **human character** and **nonhuman**, and the word **feasible** simply does not fit in that context. In sentence **2**, the choice of the words **man-machine interface** is puzzling, and in sentence **3**, the choice of **economy** is confusing.

The other sample sentences are examples of confusing or puzzling sentences produced by faulty syntax (arrangement of words). The writers of those sentences started out on a certain track but got derailed, or they switched to another track. Sentence **1**, for instance, starts out well enough—**In these particular cases that I have heard about**—but then gets derailed. Sentence **4** starts out on one track and then switches to another.

If readers cannot figure out what the writer meant to say, they often cannot analyze what went wrong with the sentence, and they certainly cannot suggest how the bewildering sentence might be fixed up. The best they can do is to point out that the sentence makes no sense and urge the writer to rephrase it.

In the revisions of the sample sentences above, (1) a

guess has been made about what the author meant to say, (2) as many of the original words as possible have been retained, and (3) none of the needed stylistic changes have been made. We have merely tried to repair the sentences so that they make sense.

If reading your sentences aloud does not help you detect confusing or puzzling sentences, you may have to read them aloud to someone else.

33

33 Proper Form of Verb

Use the proper form of the verb.

Examples of the wrong form of the verb:

1. We analyzed the data and concluded that our inferences **are** logical.

rewrite:
We analyzed the data and concluded that our inferences **were** logical.

2. The dog, angry at **being woken up**, won't let the cow eat any hay, even though the dog doesn't want the hay for itself.

rewrite:
The dog, angry at **being awakened**, won't let the cow eat any hay, even though the dog doesn't want the hay for itself.

3. Hence, much effort **has went** into the design of this traffic-control system.

rewrite:
Hence, much effort **has gone** into the design of this traffic-control system.

4. Before this change was made in the work schedule, some workers **use** to arrive a half hour before the plant gates were opened.

rewrite:

> Before this change was made in the work schedule, some workers **used** to arrive a half hour before the plant gates were opened.

5. Yesterday, when the foreman left his glasses **laying** on the workbench, he walked off without them.

rewrite:

> Yesterday, when the foreman left his glasses **lying** on the workbench, he walked off without them.

6. A few weeks before fall quarter **begans**, the first-year students have their first exposure to college life.

rewrite:

> A few weeks before fall quarter **begins**, the first-year students have their first exposure to college life.

Native speakers of English are often not aware of how subtly complicated the English verb system is, especially the system of tenses, which indicates the *time* of an action or a state of being. But foreigners who have to learn English in school are painfully aware of the subtleties of the verb system. English is doubly difficult for those foreigners whose native languages do not have a system of tenses for their verbs. Instead of indicating time by making some change in the *form* of the verb (e.g., **walk**, **walked**; **sleep**, **slept**), these languages indicate time by adding some word to the sentence—as English sometimes does to indicate future time, even when the verb indicates present time (e.g., **She goes tomorrow**).

Native speakers of English, who learn the language in the natural way, as part of the normal process of growing up, usually handle the complicated verb system quite well. Occasionally, however, most of us use the wrong form of a verb, as did the writers of the sample sentences above. Let us analyze and correct the sample sentences and then review some of the basic conventions governing the formation of the past tense and the past participle of the English verb.

The omission of the **-d** at the end of **use** in sentence **4** is understandable, because in speaking, we are scarcely conscious of pronouncing the final **-d**. But this expression must always be written as **used to**. In sentence **3**, the writer has used the wrong form of the main verb with the auxiliary verb **has** (**has went** instead of **has gone**). In the *when* clause of sentence **5**, the writer has used the incorrect transitive verb **laying** for the correct intransitive verb **lying**.

Sentence **1** illustrates the error known as **faulty sequence of tenses**—that is, a needless or an unjustifiable shift of the tenses of the verbs in successive clauses or sentences. In sentence **1**, the writer has used two past tenses, **analyzed** and **concluded**, but in the noun clause beginning with the word **that** has inexplicably used the present tense of the verb, **are**, instead of the past tense, **were**. In sentence **2**, the writer has used the wrong form (**being woken up**) of the past tense of the verbal. The correct form in that sentence is **being awakened**.

Most of the errors that writers make with verbs involve the lack of agreement in person or number between the subject and predicate or the wrong past-tense form or the wrong past-participle form. Subject-predicate agreement is dealt with in **22**. This section has dealt mainly with improper past-tense and past-participle forms. The majority of English verbs form their past tense and past participle by adding **-ed** or **-d** to the stem form (e.g., **walk**, **walked**; **believe**, **believed**). These verbs are called *regular verbs* or sometimes *weak verbs*.

The so-called *irregular verbs* or *strong verbs* form their past tense and past participle by means of a change in spelling (e.g., **sing**, **sang**, **sung**; **hide**, **hid**, **hidden**). Most

33

native speakers of English know the principal parts of most of these irregular verbs. When they do not know, or are not sure of, the principal parts, they consult a good dictionary, which supplies the past tense and past participle of all irregular verbs. But for your convenience, the principal parts of some of the most commonly used irregular verbs are presented on the following page. (Incidentally, the *stem form* of the verb is the form that combines with *to* to become the infinitive—**to walk**, **to go**; the stem form is also the form that the verb has when it is used with the first-person pronouns in the present tense—**I walk**, **we go**.)

33

PRINCIPAL PARTS OF SOME IRREGULAR VERBS

stem form	past tense form	past-participle form
begin	began	begun
bite	bit	bitten
blow	blew	blown
break	broke	broken
choose	chose	chosen
do	did	done
drink	drank	drunk
drive	drove	driven
eat	ate	eaten
fall	fell	fallen
fly	flew	flown
forget	forgot	forgotten
give	gave	given
go	went	gone
know	knew	known
lay	laid	laid
lie	lay	lain
pay	paid	paid
ride	rode	ridden
ring	rang	rung
rise	rose	risen
run	ran	run
see	saw	seen
sit	sat	sat
speak	spoke	spoken
swear	swore	sworn
take	took	taken
throw	threw	thrown
wear	wore	worn

33

STYLE

Style is the result of the choices that we make from the available vocabulary and syntactical resources of our language. We may not choose—or should not choose:

- **Words and structures that are not part of the language.**

  The defendants have **klinded** the case to the Supreme Court.

  (*no such word in the English language*)

  All gas stations **have being closed** for the duration of the emergency.

  (*no such verb structure in the English language*)

- **Words and structures that make no sense.**

  The mountains lucidly transgressed sentient rocks.

  (*a grammatical but nonsensical sentence*)

- **Words and structures that do not convey a clear, unambiguous meaning.**

  The teacher gave the papers to the students that were chosen by the committee.

  (*Was it the **papers** or the **students** that were chosen by the committee?*)

Aside from these unavailable or inadvisable choices, however, the rich vocabulary and the flexible syntax of the English language offer you a number of alternative but synonymous ways of saying something. For instance, you may choose to use an active verb or a passive verb:

He reported the accident to the police.

or

The accident was reported by him to the police.

Or you may shift the position of some modifiers:

He reported the accident to the police when he was ready.

or

When he was ready, he reported the accident to the police.

Or you may substitute synonymous words and phrases:

He informed the police about the accident at the intersection.

or

John notified Sergeant James Murphy about the collision at the corner of Fifth and Main.

A number of other stylistic choices may be open to you:

(a) whether to write a long sentence or to break up the sentence into a series of short sentences.

(*long sentence*)

In a sense, we did not have history until the invention of the alphabet, because before that invention, the records of national events could be preserved only if there were bards inspired enough to sing about those events and audiences patient enough to listen to a long, metered recitation.

or

(*a series of short sentences*)

In a sense, we did not have history until the invention of the alphabet. Before that invention, the records of national events were passed on by singing bards. But those bards had to have audiences patient enough to listen to a long, metered recitation.

(b) whether to write a compound sentence or to subordinate one of the clauses.

(compound sentence)

None of the elegies that were delivered at funerals in eighteenth-century village churches have been preserved, but the "short and simple annals of the poor" have been preserved on thousands of gravestones from that era.

or

(subordinate one of the clauses)

Although none of the elegies that were delivered at funerals in eighteenth-century village churches have been preserved, the "short and simple annals of the poor" have been preserved on thousands of gravestones from that era.

(c) whether to modify a noun with an adjective clause or with a participial phrase or merely with an adjective.

(adjective clause)

The house, which was painted a garish red, did not find a buyer for two months.

or

(participial phrase)

The house, painted a garish red, did not find a buyer for two months.

or

(adjective)

The garishly red house did not find a buyer for two months.

(d) whether to use literal language or figurative language.

(literal)

The president walked into a room filled with angry reporters.

or

(figurative)

The president walked into a hornet's nest.

(e) whether to use a learned word or an ordinary word (*altercation* or *quarrel*), a specific word or a general word (*sauntered* or *walked*), a formal word or a colloquial word (*children* or *kids*).

(*polysyllabic, formal words*)
Everyone was astonished by her phenomenal equanimity.

or

(*colloquial words*)
Everyone was flabbergasted by her unusual cool.

or

(*ordinary words*)
Everyone was surprised by her composure.

(f) whether to begin a succession of sentences with the same word and the same structure or to vary the diction and the structure.

(*same word, same structure*)
We wanted to preserve our heritage. We wanted to remind our children of our national heroes. We wanted to inspire subsequent generations to emulate our example.

or

(*different words, different structures*)
We wanted to preserve our heritage. Our children, in turn, needed to be reminded of our national heroes. Could we inspire subsequent generations to emulate our example?

The availability of options such as these gives us the opportunity to achieve variety in our style. *By varying the length, the rhythm, and the structure of our sentences, we can avoid monotony, an attention-deadening quality in prose.* The previous sentence is a good example of the variety made possible by the availability of options. All the meanings packed into that sentence could be laid out in a series of short sentences:

We vary the length of our sentences.
We vary the rhythm of our sentences.
We vary the structure of our sentences.
We can avoid monotony.
Monotony in prose deadens the attention of readers.

But by a series of transformations that involve **combining** (compounding), **embedding** (subordinating), **shifting** (rearranging), or **deleting** (omitting), we can produce a single neat sentence that emphasizes the main idea and holds the readers' attention. Here is one way that we might have chosen to express all the meanings contained in the five short sentences above:

If we vary the length, the rhythm, and the structure of our sentences, we can avoid monotony, which deadens readers' attention.

The italicized sentence on the previous page represents another way in which all the meanings in the five short sentences could be expressed. By using a different blend of combining, embedding, shifting, and deleting, we could come up with still other ways of expressing all the meanings. The different ways result in different styles.

Choice is the key word in connection with style. Some choices we may not, or should not, make. As was pointed out at the beginning of this section, we may not choose what the grammar of the language does not allow. Furthermore, we cannot choose resources of language that we do not command. We would also be ill-advised to choose words and structures that are inappropriate for the subject matter, the occasion, or the audience.

Aside from those constraints, however, we have hundreds of decisions to make about the choice of vocabulary or syntax while writing. Grammar will determine whether a particular stylistic choice is *correct*—that is, whether a particular locution complies with the conventions of the language. Rhetoric will determine whether a particular stylistic choice is *effective*—that is, whether a particular locution conveys the intended meaning with the clarity, economy, emphasis, and tone appropriate to the subject matter, occasion, audience, and desired effect.

The previous section dealt with what the grammar of the language permits—or, more accurately, with what the conventions of Edited American English permit. This section on style will guide writers in making judicious choices from among the available options. Questions about style are not so much questions about *right* and *wrong* as questions about *good, better, best.*

40

40 Wrong Word/Faulty Predication

Choose the right word or expressions for what you intend to say.

Examples of wrong words or expressions.

1. Before we **dwell** deeply into the physics of laser beams, we need to review the most recent literature on the subject.

rewrite:

Before we **delve** deeply into the physics of laser beams, we need to review the most recent literature on the subject.

2. By adopting this system, the Parking Division would **receive less hassles** and more **appraisal**.

rewrite:

By adopting this system, the Parking Division would **experience fewer hassles** and **gain more approval**.

3. This survey **does have** justified criticisms.

rewrite:

This survey **can be justifiably criticized.**

4. As mentioned earlier, this method mimics the problem-solving techniques used by scientists, a desirable **trait** in any expert system.

rewrite:

As mentioned earlier, this method mimics the problem-solving techniques used by scientists, a desirable **approach** in any expert system.

5. This project **has high expectations** of success.

rewrite:

We confidently **expect** this project to succeed.

6. An exemplary fuel system **is when** you get maximum efficiency at minimum cost.

rewrite:

An exemplary fuel sytem **is one** that provides maximum efficiency at minimum cost.

7. The reason she failed the examination **is because** she was sick at the time.

rewrite:

The reason she failed the examination **is that** she was sick at the time.

8. The beach **is where** I get my worst sunburn.

rewrite:

The beach **is the place** where I get my worst sunburn.

A word is labeled "wrong" when it does not express the author's intended meaning. The most obvious instances of a "wrong word" is the substitution, usually due to carelessness, of a homonym (a like-sounding word) for the intended word—e.g., **through** for **threw**, **there** for **their**, **sole** for **soul**, **loose** for **lose**, **here** for **hear**.

Another kind of "wrong word" is called a **malaproprism**, after Mrs. Malaprop in Richard Sheridan's play *The Rivals*. Mrs. Malaprop would says things like "as headstrong as an *allegory* on the banks of the Nile," when she should have used the word *alligator*. There is something like a malaproprism in sentence **1**: the author used the like-sounding verb **dwell** for the right verb **delve**.

Another kind of "wrong word" is found in sentence **4**. In the appositive that ends this sentence, **a desirable trait in any expert system**, the author has used the word **trait**. There is some ambiguity about whether the word **trait** is in apposition with **method** or **techniques**, but in either case, a **method** or a **technique** cannot be referred to as a **trait**. In the revision of this sentence, the word **approach** has been substituted for **trait**.

Sentences **2**, **3**, **5**, **6**, **7**, **8** illustrate faulty predications. In sentence **2**, for instance, the verb **receive** is not compatible with both **hassles** and **appraisal**. We have substituted the verb **experience** to go with **hassles** and have used the verb **gained** to go with **appraisal**. But **appraisal** is obviously a wrong word here, and **less** is the wrong word to go with the countable noun **hassles**. So we have substituted **approvals** for **appraisal** and **fewer** for **less**.

In sentence **3**, the verb **does have** is not a proper predication for the subject **survey**. We have changed the predicate to **can be justifiably criticized**. Likewise, in sentence **5**, the predication **has high expectations** does not fit with the subject **project**. We have revised that sentence to read as follows: **We confidently expect this project to succeed**.

Sentences **6**, **7**, and **8** illustrate common instances of faulty predication involving a syntactical mismatch between the subject and the predicate. The adverb clauses in those sentences cannot serve as complements for the verb **to be**. (No more could a simple adverb serve as the complement of the verb **to be**: "He is swiftly.") One way to correct such faulty predications is to put some kind of nominal

40

structure after the **to be** verb—a noun, a noun phrase, or a noun clause (see the revisions of sentences **6**, **7**, and **8**). Avoid this kind of predication:

> The reason is because . . .
>
> An example is when . . .
>
> A ghetto is where . . .

41 Inexact Word

41

Choose the precise word for what you want to say.

Examples of imprecise words:

1. Most of this insurance money has been paid for **larger** accidents.

rewrite:

> Most of this insurance money has been paid for **more serious** accidents.

2. The corporation must do something about its **overwhelming ability** to lose money.

rewrite:

> The corporation must do something about its **persistent tendency** to lose money.

3. With the data gathered in my research, I will formulate a safety program that will be **more competent** than the one we now have.

rewrite:

> With the data gathered in my research, I will formulate a safety program that will be **more reliable** than the one we now have.

4. Integrity is a **thing** that everyone admires.

rewrite:

> Integrity is a **virtue** that everyone admires.

5. I liked the movie *Presumed Innocent* because it was **interesting**.

rewrite:

I liked the movie *Presumed Innocent* because it was **suspenseful**.

6. John cashed his government bonds, **as** he was about to go on his summer vacation.

rewrite:

John cashed his government bonds **because** he was about to go on his summer vacation.

Whereas a "wrong word" misses the target entirely, an "imprecise word" hits all around the bull's-eye and never on dead center. The governing principle here is that we should strive only for as much precision in diction as the situation demands.

In the spoken medium, diction is often imprecise. Fortunately, in many conversational situations, our diction does not have to be sharply precise in order to communicate adequately. In a conversation, for instance, if someone asked, "How did you like him?" we might respond, "Oh, I thought he was very nice." The word *nice* does not convey a precise meaning, but for the particular situation, it may be precise enough. The word *nice* here, reinforced by our tone of voice, certainly conveys the message that we approve of the person, that we are favorably disposed toward the person. In speech, we do not have the leisure to search for the words that express our meaning exactly. If the person who asked the question was not satisfied with our general word of approval, *nice*, that person could ask us to be more specific about what we meant.

In the written medium, however, we do have the leisure to search for a precise word, and we are not available to the reader who may want or need more specific information than our words supply. Generally, the written medium requires that the words we choose be as exact, as specific, as unequivocal as we can make them. Consulting a thesaurus

41

or, better yet, a dictionary that discriminates the meanings of synonyms will frequently yield the word that conveys our intended meaning precisely.

The word *interesting* in sentence 5 is too general to convey a precise meaning. A reader's response to a general word like that would be to ask, "In what way was the movie interesting?" If the writer had written "exciting" or "thought-provoking" or "suspenseful," readers might want more particulars, but at least they would have a clearer idea of the sense in which the writer of that sentence found the movie *interesting*.

In the oral medium, we can get by with a catchall word like **thing**, as in sentence 4, but writing allows us the leisure to search for a word that will serve as a more accurate predicate for **integrity**. We can choose a word like **policy**, **habit**, **disposition**, **virtue**—whichever word fits best with what we want to say about honesty here.

The writer of sentence 2 may intend to be ironic when he or she speaks about an **overwhelming ability**. Both of the words in that phrase are positive, but losing money and being rated as high risk by insurance companies are negative qualities. There would have been more of a matchup between the words and the qualities if the writer had used the phrase **a persistent tendency**. In sentence 3, **more reliable** would be a more exact predication to apply to **a safety program** than the phrase **more competent**. Likewise, in sentence 1, **catastrophic** or **serious** would be a more precise adjective to apply to **accidents** than the adjective **large**.

The subordinating conjunction **as** carries a variety of meanings, and it is not always possible to tell from the context which of its several meanings it carries in a particular sentence. In sentence 6, we cannot tell whether **as** is being used in its sense of "because" or "since" or "when" or "while." We should use the conjunction that exactly expresses our intended meaning: **when** he was about to go on his vacation or **because** he was about to go on his vacation—or whatever conjunction best says what we want to say. In the rewrite, we chose the subordinating conjunction **because**. Reserve the conjunction **as** for those contexts in which there is no possibility of ambiguity, as in sentences like "In that kind of situation, he acts exactly as he should" and "Do as I say."

42 Inappropriate Word

Choose words that are appropriate to the context.

Examples of inappropriate words:

1. These readings give us a **feel** for how precise this measuring system is.

   rewrite:
   These readings give us a **sense** of how precise this measuring system is.

2. He did not want to **exacerbate** his mother's **sangfroid**, so he **indited** an **epistolary message** to inform her of his unavoidable **retardation**.

   rewrite:
   He did not want to **upset** his mother, so he **wrote** her a **note** to inform her that he would be **late**.

3. The judge ruled that the **kids** should be assigned to a foster home.

   rewrite:
   The judge ruled that the **children** should be assigned to a foster home.

4. The staff of the mayor's office were **freaked out** by the financial officer's budget report.

rewrite:

> The staff of the mayor's office were **disconcerted** by the financial officer's budget report.

A word is inappropriate if it does not fit—if it is out of tune with—the subject matter, the occasion, the audience, or the personality of the writer. It is a word that is conspicuously "out of place" in its environment.

No word in isolation can be labeled inappropriate; a word must be seen in the company of other words. Because technical writing often necessitates the use of specialized terminology, the diction in that kind of discourse may strike the uninitiated reader as being flagrantly inappropriate. But in the context of that kind of writing and for its audience, the jargon may very well be quite appropriate. What we are talking about in this section is the kind of word-choice that is "out of place" or "out of tune" in its context.

Sentence 2 exhibits the kind of language used by writers who are passing through a phase in which they seem unable to say even a simple thing in a simple way. Beginning writers consciously striving to enlarge their vocabulary often produce sentences like this one. Instead of using a thesaurus to find an accurate or an appropriate word, they use it to find an unusual or a polysyllabic word that they think will impress their readers. The label sometimes applied to such pretentious, ornate diction is "purple prose" or "gobbledygook." Fortunately, most of those who are ambitious enough to want to expand their working vocabulary eventually develop enough sophistication to be able to judge when the language they choose is appropriate and when it is not. See the conversion in sentence 2 into more ordinary language.

Sentences 3 and 4 exhibit the opposite kind of inappropriate language: language that is too colloquial, too informal, for its occasion or audience. In sentence 4,

freaked out is too colloquial for its context. **Disconcert**, the substitute verb for **freak out**, is not the kind of word that is part of most people's everyday vocabulary, especially in the speech medium, but it is a word that fits better with the surrounding words than the slang term does. Likewise in sentence **3**: the very common word **kids** is too colloquial for its context. The colloquial word **feel** in sentence **1** is also out of tune with its environment. The word **sense** is more suitable for that context.

Since dictionaries, thesauruses, and handbooks will not be of much help in telling you that a word is inappropriate, you will have to rely on the criteria of subject matter, occasion, audience, desired effect, and personality of the writer to guide you in making reliable judgments about the appropriateness of your word-choice. Dictionaries, for instance, give you information about the denotations of words, not about the connotations of words. Another way of putting the precept enunciated at the head of this section is to say that your "voice" must remain in harmony with the overall tone that you have established in a particular piece of writing.

43

43 Unidiomatic Expression

Use the proper idiom.

Examples of lapse of idiom:

1. **Had I didn't check** with the mathematics department about this course, I would have wasted both my time and my money.

rewrite:

> **Had I not checked** with the mathematics department about this course, I would have wasted both my time and my money.

2. I thought I would not have any problems because I **filled** my application according to the instructions circulated by the Dean's office.

rewrite:

I thought I would not have any problems because I **filled out** my application according to the instructions circulated by the Dean's office.

3. He was assigned to your company **to help you solving** some of your current problems.

rewrite:

He was assigned to your company **to help you solve** some of your current problems.

4. This report will **apprise you on** the suitability of the arboretum as the site of the trash-burning plant.

rewrite:

This report will **apprise you of** the suitability of the arboretum as the site of the trash-burning plant.

5. CSMP, which stands for "Continuous System Modeling Programs," **is program** that allows the operator to handle systems that are very complex.

rewrite:

CSMP, which stands for "Continuous System Modeling Programs," **is a program** that allows the operator to handle systems that are very complex.

To label a locution unidiomatic is to indicate that native speakers of the language do not say it that way—in any dialect of the language. Unidiomatic expressions are one of the most common weaknesses to be found in the prose of unpracticed writers. Why lapses of idiom occur so frequently is a good question to ask, because writers presumably have not heard other native speakers use the curious expressions that they write down on paper. One explanation for the frequency of idiomatic lapses is that unpracticed writers use words and structures in the written medium that they seldom or never use in speech; and because they have not paid close enough attention to the way native speakers say something, they make a guess—usually a wrong guess—at how the expression should be phrased.

No word by itself is ever unidiomatic; only combinations of words can be unidiomatic. (For that reason, more than one word in the sample sentences is put in boldface type.) The most common kind of idiomatic lapse is the one that involves a preposition in combination with some other word or words. Sentence 4 presents an example of an unidiomatic preposition. With the verb **apprise**, the native speakers do not use the preposition **on** (**apprise you on**); instead they use the preposition **of** (*apprise you of*). The **out** that is used to correct the unidiomatic expression in sentence 2 (**I filled out my application**) is sometimes a preposition, but in that sentence the **out** is a particle that goes with the verb **filled**.

In sentence 3, the structure that fits idiomatically with the infinitive **to help** is not the participial structure **solving** but the infinitive structure **[to] solve—to help you solve**.

Sentence 1 illustrates an instance of a writer using an expression that he or she had never used before. This writer does not remember just how the expression is worded and so writes, **"Had I didn't check."** The correct idiom here, **had I not checked**, is an alternative way that native speakers of English have of saying **if I had not checked**. This writer had probably heard the **had** structure being used but did not remember how the expression was worded when he or she wrote this sentence.

Sentence 5 illustrates an idiomatic lapse that foreigners often make: the lapse involving the use of the article or determiner **the** and **a** (**an**). Understandably, writers whose native language does not use articles (the Oriental lan-

43

guages, for instance) have a great deal of difficulty knowing when to put in the article and when to leave it out. Americans, for instance, say, "My daughter goes to the university" but also say, "My daughter goes to college." Why do Americans put in the article **the** with the word **university** but leave out the article **the** with the word **college**? Why, in sentence 5, do we have to put in the article before the word **program—a progam** or **the program**? There is no rational explanation for these usages. Idiom is what determines the proper usage in these instances. You simply have to attune your ear to the way that native speakers of a language say things.

What prevents a handbook from setting reliable guidelines for proper idiom is the fact that logic plays little or no part in establishing the idioms of a language. If logic were involved in establishing idioms, we would say, "He **looked down** a word in the dictionary" instead of what we do say, "He **looked up** a word in the dictionary. Editors or teachers can call your attention to an unidiomatic expression and can insert the correct idiom, but they often cannot give you rules or guidelines that will prevent other lapses of idiom. You simply have to learn the proper idioms by reading and listening attentively to the way the English language is written or spoken.

44 Trite Expression

Avoid trite expressions.

Examples of trite expressions:

1. When we finished our research, we were **tired but happy**, and that night we **slept like a log**.

rewrite:

When we finished our research, we were **exhausted but content**, and that night we **slept soundly**.

2. His expression of sympathy would **warm the cockles of one's heart**.

rewrite:

His expression of sympathy would make one **feel comforted and grateful**.

3. Convinced that the use of drugs has increased dramatically among the workers on the assembly line, this automotive company must **nip the problem in the bud** before it **runs rampant**.

rewrite:

Convinced that the use of drugs has increased dramatically among the workers on the assembly line, this automotive company must **solve the problem** before it **gets out of control**.

4. She didn't **bat an eyelash** when I told her **flat out** that she was **born with a silver spoon in her mouth**.

rewrite:

She didn't **squirm a bit** when I told her **frankly** that she was a **pampered child**.

There is nothing grammatically or idiomatically wrong with a trite expression. A trite expression is only *stylistically* objectionable—mainly because it is a *tired* expression. Whether an expression is tired is, of course, a relative matter. What is lackluster for some readers may be bright-penny new for others. But it would be surprising if the expressions in the sample sentences above were not jaded for most readers.

Trite expressions are certain combinations of words or certain figures of speech that have been used so often that they have lost their freshness and even their meaning for most readers. Rhetorically, the price you pay for using trite language is the alienation of your readers. Readers stop paying attention. You may have something new and important to say, but if your message is delivered in threadbare language, you will lose or fail to capture the attention of your readers.

Figures of speech are especially prone to staleness. Metaphors like **nip in the bud** and **slept like a log** were once fresh and cogent; now they are so wilted from overuse that we call them "dead metaphors." Trite combinations of words like **tired but happy** and **runs rampant** produce glazed-eyed readers. Other trite expressions have been uttered so often that they have become folk expressions. Every generation picks up tired expressions like the following: **the apple of one's eye, waited with bated breath, taking it on the chin, down at the heels, eat your heart out, one foot in the grave, in cold blood, knee-jerk response, right on the nose, chip on one's shoulder, toe the mark**.

Ironically, one of the ways in which to revise sentences that have trite language is to use the most familiar, ordinary language. Sentence 1, for instance, would be improved simply by using different words for the trite expression **tired but happy** (we have used the words **exhausted but content**) and by using a simple adverb like **soundly** for the simile **slept like a log**.

Sometimes, making a daring alteration in a tired expression can rejuvenate the sentence. The expression **a well-rounded education** is one of the yawn-producing clichés in our language. Look at how the following sentence is perked up by substituting a fresh expression for that stale expression:

> My primary objective in coming to college was to get a **well-squared education**.

If you make an effort to invent your own figures of speech, you may produce awkward, strained figures, but at least they will be fresh. Instead of adopting the hackneyed metaphor **nip the problem in the bud**, make up your own metaphor, such as the metaphor in the following sentence:

> Convinced now that the use of drugs has increased dramatically among workers on the assembly line, this automotive company must excise this tumor before it becomes a raging cancer.

It takes a great deal of sophistication about language for someone even to recognize trite expressions, and those who do not read very much can hardly be expected to detect tired language, because almost all the expressions that they encounter are relatively new to them. They may have to rely on others to point out the trite language in their prose.

Be wary of weary words.

45 Awkward Sentence

Rephrase awkwardly constructed sentences.

Examples of awkward sentences:

1. Hiring people with the proper education **for advising** is the key **to stopping misinforming communications**.

rewrite:

> Hiring people with the kind of education **that fits them to be an advisor** is the key **to preventing bad communications**.

2. **Uncertainty handling** is a major concern of any diagnostic system that physicians use.

rewrite:

> A major concern of any diagnostic system that physicians use should be **its capacity for handling uncertainty**.

3. Parking anywhere at night is risky, but **in the campus area on**

side streets is probably one of the most dangerous places in the city.

rewrite:

Parking anywhere at night is risky, but side streets in the campus area are probably among the most dangerous places in the city.

4. You could get a dose of the best exercise a person could undertake, walking. I believe that a person should walk at a leisurely pace, with no set goal on distance.

rewrite:

The best exercise for people is walking at a leisurely pace as far as they feel like going.

45

The fault dealt with in **32**, in the Grammar section, concerned sentences that were so badly put together that they revealed no meaning or only a vague meaning. Awkward sentences, which are dealt with in this section, are sentences so ineptly put together that they are difficult—but not impossible—for readers to understand. They are sentences that are grammatically passable but stylistically weak.

Those who write awkwardly constructed sentences are usually not aware that their sentences are clumsy; they have to be told that their sentences are clumsy. If they would adopt the practice of reading their sentences aloud, they would often detect awkward, odd-sounding combinations of words. Thus alerted, they could then examine their sentences to see whether the sentences manifest any of the usual causes of awkwardness:

(a) Excessive number of words (see sentence **4**)

(b) Words and phrases out of their normal order (note the position of **walking** in sentence **4**)

(c) A succession of prepositional phrases ("the president **of** the largest chapter **of** the national fraternity **of** students **of** mechanical engineering")

(d) Pretentious circumlocutions ("the penultimate month of the year" for "November")

(e) Split constructions ("I, chastened by my past experiences, resolved to never consciously and maliciously circulate, even if true, damaging reports about my friends.")

(f) A succession of rhyming words ("She tries wisely to revise the evidence supplied by her eyes.")

The sample sentences at the beginning of this section are awkward for a variety of reasons. By pruning some of the deadwood, rearranging some of the parts, and using simpler, more idiomatic phrases, we can improve the articulation of those clumsy sentences.

Construct your sentences so smoothly that your readers won't have to stumble through them.

46 Wordy Sentence

Cut out unnecessary words.

Examples of wordy sentences:

1. It is my overall intent to develop a safety program into a form that is superior to the old safety format.

rewrite:
   I intend to develop a safety program that is superior to the present one. (from 21 words to 14 words)

2. The meaning, at least in my own eyes, that he is trying to convey in the poem "Arms and the Boy" is of the evilness of war in that it forces innocent people to take up instruments of

death and destruction and then tries to teach them to love to use them.

rewrite:

As I see it, the poet's thesis in "Arms and the Boy" is that war is evil, because it not only forces people to take up arms but makes them love to use these weapons to kill other human beings. (from 52 words to 40 words)

3. In this modern world of today, we must get an education that will prepare us for a job in our vocation in life.

rewrite:

In the modern world, we must get an education that will prepare us for a job. (from 23 words to 16 words)

4. The prescribed weight will provide limitations for the design and use of the ladder, which when considered with the slenderness ratio will determine the ultimate design of the ladder and its components.

rewrite:

The prescribed weight and the slenderness ratio will determine the ultimate design of the ladder and its components. (from 32 words to 18 words)

A "wordy sentence" is one in which a writer has used more words than are needed to say what has to be said. The superfluous words simply clutter up the sentence and impede its movement. Speakers are especially prone to verbosity because words come so easily to their tongues. But writers too are prone to verbosity once they acquire a certain facility with words. Facile writers have to make a conscious effort to control their expenditure of words. Writers would soon learn to cultivate restraint if they were charged for every word used, as they are when they send a telegram. They should not, of course, strive for a "telegraphic" or a "headline" style, but they should learn to value words so much that they spend words sparingly.

Each of the revised sentences above uses fewer words

than the original. The reduction ranges from seven words to fourteen words. If the writers were being charged a quarter a word, they would probably find additional superfluous words to delete or would rephrase the sentence to save words.

One should not become obsessed with saving words, but one should seize every opportunity, in the revising stage, to clear out deadwood, such as the **It is my overall intent** in sentence 1. As Alexander Pope said,

> Words are like leaves, and where they most abound,
> Much fruit of sense beneath is rarely found.

47

47 Repetition

Avoid careless or needless repetition of words and ideas.

Examples of careless or needless repetition:

1. Please remain in your seat until the aircraft comes to a **complete stop** at the gate.

rewrite:
Please remain in your seat until the aircraft comes to a **stop** at the gate.

2. As to the type of equipment **requirement needed**, the engineers recommend that a bonding machine be used for the laminations.

rewrite:
As to the type of equipment **needed**, the engineers recommend that a bonding machine be used for the laminations.

3. I have faced this problem about the fatigue factor for some time now, and I have **thought** about it regularly **in my own mind**.

rewrite:

I have faced this problem about the fatigue factor for some time now, and I have **thought** about it regularly.

4. After **setting** up camp, **we set** off to watch the sun **set**.

rewrite:

After preparing camp, **we took** off to watch the sun **set**.

5. The company intends to develop a **more superior** retirement program.

rewrite:

The company intends to develop a **superior** retirement program.

6. The objective point of view accentuates the emotional intensity of the love affair and the **impending** failure that will **eventually happen**.

rewrite:

The objective point of view accentuates the emotional intensity of the love affair and its **impending** failure.

7. The hardness of the metal increased to a certain point and **then** decreased **afterwards**.

rewrite:

The hardness of the metal increased to a certain point and **then** decreased.

A "careless or needless repetition" refers either to the recurrence of a word in the same sentence or adjoining sentences or to the use of synonymous words that produce what is called a **redundancy** or a **tautology**.

The emphasis in this caution about repetition should be put on the words *careless* and *needless*, for there are cases where repetition serves a purpose. For instance, the repetition of key words can be an effective means of achieving coherence in a paragraph. And sometimes it is better to repeat a word, even in the same sentence, than to run the risk of ambiguity or misunderstanding. In the first sentence of this paragraph, for example, the word **repetition** has been repeated because the use of the pronoun *it* in the place of **repetition** would be ambiguous. (We might wonder whether that pronoun *it* referred to **emphasis** or to **repetition**.)

The boldfaced words in sentences **1**, **2**, **5**, **6**, **7** are instances of redundancy or tautology (needless repetition of the same idea in different words). In sentence **3**, the phrase **in my own mind** is superfluous (where else does one think but in the mind?). The repetition of **set** in sentence **4** is due simply to carelessness.

Repetition sometimes serves a useful purpose. However, avoid repetition when it merely adds unnecessary words to the sentence.

48

48 Figurative Language

Avoid mixed metaphors.

Examples of mixed metaphors:

1. When we tried to get our proposal **off the ground**, we found that it **sank in a sea of apathy**.

rewrite:
    When we tried to get our proposal **off the ground**, we found that it did not **get up enough speed to become airborne**.

2. In "The Dead," James Joyce uses small talk as an effective **weapon** to **illustrate** his thesis.

rewrite:
    In "The Dead," James Joyce uses small talk as a **mirror** to **reflect** his thesis.

3. The extraordinary success of this project struck a **spark** that **massaged** the team's enthusiasm.

rewrite:
> The extraordinary success of this project struck a **spark** that **ignited** the team's enthusiasm.

4. The manager tried **to scale the wall** of their indifference but found that he could not **burrow** through it.

rewrite:
> The manager tried **to scale the wall** of their indifference but found that he could not **surmount** it.

48

A mixed metaphor is the result of a writer's failure to keep a consistent image in mind. All metaphors are based on the perceived likenesses between things that exist in different orders of being—as for instance between a *man* and a *greyhound* ("The lean shortstop is a greyhound when he runs the bases"), *fame* and a *spur* ("Fame is the spur to ambition"), *mail* and an *avalanche* ("The mail buried the staff under an avalanche of complaints"). Whenever any detail is incompatible with one or more terms of the analogy, the metaphor is said to be mixed.

In the first part of sentence 1, the image we get is that of an airplane taking off, but in the second half of the sentence, the image changes to that of a ship sinking. If one were climbing (**scaling**) a wall (see sentence 4), one could not at the same time dig (**burrow**) through it. A **spark** could start a fire, but it could not **massage** anything (see sentence 3). A **weapon** could wound someone, but a **weapon** could not **illustrate** something (see sentence 2).

Figures of speech lend color and vivacity to your style. And for that reason, you should cultivate their use. But remember that when you resort to poetic analogies, forming and maintaining a clear picture of the notion you are attempting to express figuratively will ensure a consistent metaphor.

49 Passive Verb

Consider whether an active verb would be preferable to a passive verb.

Examples of questionable use of the passive voice:

1. Because of the increasing use in automobiles of inflatable restraints (air bags), much testing **is required** of carmakers to ensure a correct and reliable operation of this system.

rewrite:

Because of the increasing use in automobiles of inflatable restraints (air bags), carmakers **must do** a great deal of testing to ensure a correct and reliable operation of this system.

2. Money **was borrowed** by us so that it could pay off the mortgage on our home.

rewrite:

We **borrowed** money so that we could pay off the mortgage on our home.

3. From these recurrent images of hard, resistant metals, it **can be inferred** by us that her husband is a mechanical, heartless person.

rewrite:

From these recurrent images of hard, resistant metals, we **can infer** that her husband is a mechanical, heartless person.

4. By asking a multitude of probing questions, she **was overwhelmed** by the government examiner.

rewrite:

By asking a multitude of probing questions, the government examiner **overwhelmed** her.

If the use of a passive verb is questionable, it is questionable stylistically, not grammatically. To question the use of a passive verb is to ask the writer to consider whether the sentence would not be more emphatic or more economical or less awkward or somehow "neater" if an active verb were used. Challenged to consider the option available in a particular sentence, the writer must be the final judge of the best choice in that case.

Writers sometimes decide to use the passive verb because they want to give special emphasis to some word in the sentence. In sentence **2**, for instance, the word **money** gets special emphasis because it occupies the initial position. If an active verb is used in that sentence, however—as it is in the revision—the word **we** gets the special emphasis. The writer's choice of an active or a passive verb in that sentence may depend on where he or she wants to put the emphasis.

It would be more difficult for the writers of sentences **1** and **3** to cite emphasis as the justification for their choices of the passive verb. Writers can also justify the use of a passive verb when they do not know the agent of an action or prefer not to reveal the agent or consider it unnecessary to indicate the agent, as in a sentence such as "The story was reported to all the newspapers."

Dangling verbals often result from the use of a passive verb in the main clause of a sentence (see **25** on dangling verbals in the Grammar section). The context of sentence **4** suggests that the lead-off gerund phrase (**By asking. . .**) may be dangling—that is, that it was not the woman (**she**) but the **government examiner** who was asking a multitude of questions. If the examiner was the questioner, the writer of that sentence may not choose the passive verb for the main clause but must use the active verb.

The use of a passive verb is *not* forbidden. But the writer should always be prepared to consider whether the use of a passive verb is justifiable in a particular sentence.

PARAGRAPHING

One way to regard paragraphing is to view it as a system of punctuating stages of thought presented in units larger than the word and the sentence. Paragraphing is a means of alerting readers to a shift of focus in the development of the main idea of the whole discourse. It marks off for the reader's convenience the individually distinct but related parts of the whole discourse. How paragraphing facilitates reading would be made dramatically evident if a whole discourse were written or printed—as ancient manuscripts once were—in a single, unbroken block.

Like punctuation and mechanics, paragraphing is a feature only of the written language. Some linguists claim that speakers of connected discourse signal their "paragraphs" by pauses and by shifts in the tone of their voice. (The next time you hear a speech being delivered from a written text, see if you can detect when the speaker shifts to another paragraph of his or her text.) But speakers are not conscious—especially in extemporaneous stretches of talk—of paragraphing the stream of sound as writers must be when they are writing their manuscripts.

The typographical device most commonly used to mark off paragraphs is *indentation*. The first line of each new paragraph starts several spaces (usually five spaces on the typewriter) from the left-hand margin. Another convention for marking paragraphs is the block system: beginning the first line at the left-hand margin but leaving double or triple spacing between paragraphs. One of the forms of writing that regularly uses the block system is the single-spaced, typewritten business letter.

In this section, only three aspects of the paragraph are treated: unity, coherence, and adequate development. The traditional means of developing the central idea of a paragraph are mentioned in the section on adequate development, but they are not discussed at length. The means of developing paragraphs are fundamentally a concern of invention, which is the province of a rhetoric text rather than of a handbook. However, if you take care of unity, coherence, and adequate development, you will be attending to the three most persistent problems that beset the composition of written paragraphs.

50 Unity

Preserve the unity of the paragraph.

The principle governing paragraph unity is that a paragraph should develop a single topic or thesis, which is often—but not always—announced in a topic sentence. Every sentence in the paragraph should contribute in some way to the development of that single idea. When writers introduce other ideas into the paragraph, they violate the unity of the paragraph and disorient their readers.

Example of a paragraph lacking unity:

1. The eminence of Samuel Johnson inclines modern scholars to study his thoughts and opinions. His multifarious knowledge intrigued his contemporaries. Although he manifested his in-

terest in the drama by editing Shakespeare, he did not enjoy the theater. He was envious too of his former pupil David Garrick, the greatest actor of the eighteenth century.

The first sentence of paragraph 1, which has the air of being a "topic sentence," mentions that modern scholars have turned their attention to a study of Samuel Johnson. Instead of the second sentence going on to develop that idea, it mentions what Dr. Johnson meant to his contemporaries. The third sentence talks about his attitude toward drama and the theater. The fourth sentence mentions his envy of his former pupil David Garrick. What we have in this paragraph is four topics. A whole paragraph or paper could be devoted to the development of each of these four topics, but here all four of these disparate topics are packed into a single paragraph.

The following presents *one* of the ways in which the paragraph might be revised to give it unity:

> The eminence of Samuel Johnson inclines modern scholars to study his thoughts and opinions. A number of recent books and articles have dealt with his viewpoints on a variety of his interests. One of those interests was the drama. Curiously, however, although he manifested this interest by writing his own play for the stage and by editing all the plays of Shakespeare, he did not enjoy the theater. Some modern scholars have speculated that he did not enjoy the theater because of his poor eyesight and impaired hearing. Others have speculated that he disliked the theater because he was jealous of his former pupil David Garrick, who very early in his career acquired the reputation of being the greatest actor of his day.

Here is another example of a paragraph lacking unity:

2. Priests are still in great demand today because of the rapid increase of population in the United States and in other parts of the world. The Catholic Church is losing many possible followers because it does not have enough "teachers" to guide

50

those who want to become part of some religion. The Pope has been very adamant about keeping the laws that have existed for centuries. These laws prohibit the ordination of married men and women. The times have changed, and the job that was once held in high esteem is now in search of applicants. The Catholic Church needs to reconsider some of its outmoded laws.

Paragraph 2 has a certain unity: each sentence is saying something about the desperate need for more Catholic priests to serve the growing population. But it is difficult to discern the thread that stitches all of the sentences into a unit. If the first sentence was the intended topic sentence, the paragraph would have to take on a different shape than it now has. But since most of the sentences are talking about the *causes* of the current shortage of priests, it seems likely that the intended topic of the paragraph is implicit in a combination of the first and second sentences. We could give this paragraph some unity by devising a topic sentence that can serve as an umbrella for all of the other sentences in the paragraph. Here is a revision of paragraph 2:

The rapid increase of population throughout the world has created a great demand for priests, but the supply of priests has declined dramatically in the last fifty years or so. Consequently, the Catholic Church has been losing many potential followers because it does not have enough "teachers" to guide those who want to become part of some religion. One reason for the marked decline in the number of applicants for the priesthood is that the Pope has been very adamant about keeping the age-old laws that prohibit the ordination of married men and women. The inadequate supply of priests will probably persist as long as the Church refuses to reconsider these outmoded laws.

Here is a third example of a disunified paragraph:

3. Dr. Rockwell let his feelings be known on only one subject: the administration. He felt that the administrative system was out-

dated. Abolishing grades, giving the student a voice in administration, and revamping the curriculum were three steps he felt should be taken to improve the system. Dr. Rockwell taught in this manner. In class, a mysterious aura surrounded him. He was "hip" to what was going on, but he preferred to hear the members of the class rather than himself. He was quiet and somewhat shy. His eyes caught everything that went on in class. His eyes generated a feeling of understanding.

Paragraph 3 also has a certain unity: each sentence in the paragraph is talking about the teacher Dr. Rockwell. And there is a tight unity in the first three sentences: each of these sentences talks about Dr. Rockwell's attitude toward the administration. But with the fourth sentence of the paragraph, the writer introduces another and unrelated topic: a description of how Dr. Rockwell conducted himself in the classroom. If the writer had broken up this stretch of prose into two paragraphs and had reorganized some of the sentences, each of the two paragraphs would have had its own unity:

50

> Dr. Rockwell let his feelings be known on only one subject: the administration. His estimation of the administrative system of the school was largely negative. He felt, for instance, that the administrative system was outdated. Abolishing grades, giving students a voice in administration, and revamping the curriculum were three steps he felt should be taken to improve the system.
>
> Dr. Rockwell's demeanor in the classroom was remarkable. Although there was a mysterious aura about him, he was always "hip" to what was going on. His eyes caught everything that went on in class, but they generated a feeling of understanding. Even though he was a learned scholar, this quiet, somewhat shy man preferred to listen to the members of the class rather than himself.

A paragraph will have unity, will have "oneness," if every sentence in it has an obvious bearing on the development of a single topic. When writers sense that they have shifted to the discussion of another topic, they should begin a new paragraph.

51   Coherence

Compose the paragraph so that it reads coherently.

Coherence is that quality which makes it easy for a reader to follow a writer's train of thought from sentence to sentence and from paragraph to paragraph. Coherence facilitates reading because it ensures that the reader will be able to detect the relationship of the parts of a discourse. It also reflects the clear thinking of the writer because it results from the writer's arrangement of ideas in some kind of perceptible order and from the writer's use of those verbal devices that help to stitch thoughts together. In short, as the Latin roots of the word suggest (*co*, "together," + *haerēre*, "to stick"), coherence helps the parts of a discourse to "stick together."

Here are some ways to achieve coherence in a paragraph (not all of these devices, of course, have to be used in every paragraph):

(a) Repeat key words from sentence to sentence or use recognizable synonyms for key words.

(b) Use pronouns for key nouns. (Because a pronoun gets its meaning from the noun to which it refers, it is by its very nature one of those devices that help to stitch sentences together.)

(c) Use demonstrative adjectives, "pointing words" (**this** statement, **that** plan, **these** developments, **those** disasters).

(d) Use conjunctive adverbs, "thought-connecting words" (e.g., **however**, **moreover**, **also**, **nevertheless**, **therefore**, **thus**, **subsequently**, **indeed**, **then**, **accordingly**).

(e) Arrange the sequence of sentences in some kind of perceptible order (for instance, a **time order**, as in a narrative of what happened or in an explanation of how to do something; a **space order**, as in the description of a physical object or a scene; a **logical order**, such as cause to effect, effect to cause, general to particular, particular to general, whole to part, familiar to unfamiliar).

Here is an example of an incoherent paragraph:

> After the program has been written, each line is punched onto a card. The deck of cards is known as the "program source deck." The next step is to load the program compiler into the computer. The "compiler" is a program written in machine language for a particular computer, which reads the source deck and performs a translation of the program language into machine language. The machine language, in the form of instructions, is punched onto cards. This machine-language deck of cards is known as the "object deck." After the object deck has been punched, the programmer is then able to execute his program. The program is run by loading the object deck into the computer. The run of the program marks the end of the second step.

This paragraph attempts to describe an earlier form of computer programming, a description that many readers would find difficult to follow because they are not familiar with the process. But the description would be doubly difficult for those readers because it is not presented coherently. What makes this description especially difficult to follow is that the writer is doing two things at once in the paragraph: (1) designating the chronological sequence of steps in the process and (2) defining technical terms used in the description of the process. It would have been better if the writer had devoted one paragraph to defining such

51

terms as **program source deck, compiler, object deck**. Then the writer could have devoted another paragraph exclusively to the description of the process of "running a program"—first you do this, then you do that, after that you do this, etc. As the paragraph now stands, readers get lost because they are kept bouncing back and forth between definition of the terms and description of the process.

Here is one way to revise that incoherent paragraph:

Before you can understand the process of "running a program," you need some definitions of technical terms. After the program discussed in the previous paragraph has been written, each line of that program is punched onto an IBM card. The collection of these cards is known as the "program source deck." Another set of cards is known as the "compiler." The compiler "reads" the source deck and translates it into machine language, which is then punched onto IBM cards. The machine-language deck of cards that results from the operation of the compiler is known as the "object deck."

The first step in the process is to put the program source deck into the computer. Then, in order to translate the program language of the source deck into machine language, the compiler set must be inserted. Following that step, the object deck, with its instructions written out in machine language, is put into the computer. Now the program is ready to be "run" through the computer.

Here are two more examples of incoherent paragraphs:

1. The first stanza of "The Echoing Green" does not correspond with any other poem by William Blake. The glory of nature's beauty is presented in vivid details. Emotional intensity is the overall effect of the poem. Blake resents the mechanization that has been brought about by the Industrial Revolution. The rhythm of the verses contributes to the meditative mood.

51

2. As a young athlete, I played many sports, and baseball was my favorite. I never wanted to stop playing the game. I wanted to become a professional athlete like Willie Stargell or Roberto Clemente. During the time I played, the people who coached me were major influences on me, both on and off the field. The coaches would teach me and give me tips to improve my baseball skills and techniques. My coaches taught me discipline and respect, which I use in everyday situations. After my time as a baseball player was over, I continued to be a fan of the game. I watched baseball and softball games as much as I could. As I watched the games, I noticed a lack of knowledge and ability on the part of some of the coaches. The lack of knowledge and ability bothered me because these coaches were not able to bring out the potential of the young athletes. The young athletes between the ages of eight and twelve are very impressionable, and they need role models who can influence them for the rest of their lives.

51

It is difficult to suggest ways of revising paragraphs 1 and 2 because they are so incoherent that it is almost impossible to discover the principal points that the writers wanted to put across in them. If we could confer with the writers and ask them what the main idea of their paragraph was supposed to be, we could then advise them about which sentences contributed to the development of the idea (and which sentences had to be dropped because they threatened the unity of the paragraph), about the order of the sentences in the given paragraph, and about the kinds of words that would help them to knit the sequence of sentences together.

Each of the following revisions constitutes one of a number of ways in which the two paragraphs might be written to give them some coherence:

1. It is interesting to note how William Blake achieves the emotional intensity that he does in "The Echoing Green." He

achieves that intensity partly by presenting the glory of nature in vivid details that contrast with the dull, gray mechanization of the urban scene that has been produced by the Industrial Revolution. The slow rhythm of the verses also contributes to the emotional intensity by creating a meditative mood. The extraordinary collection of images in the first stanza of the poem also serves to exert a strong emotional effect on the reader.

2. As a young athlete, I played many sports, but baseball was my favorite. I liked baseball so much that I wanted to become a professional athlete, like Willie Stargell or Roberto Clemente. One of the reasons I liked baseball so much is that my coaches had a great influence on me, both on and off the field. On the field, they helped me improve my baseball skills, and off the field, they also taught me discipline and respect, which I still use in everyday situations. Their influence on me was so great that even after I stopped being an active player, I continued to watch baseball and softball games. But one thing I noticed as I watched these games was the lack of knowledge and skills manifested by the coaches. Because of the ineptness of these coaches, the highly impressionable young athletes who played for these role models were not influenced, as I was, for the rest of their lives.

Coherence is a difficult writing skill to master, but until you acquire at least a measure of that skill, you will continue to be frustrated in your efforts to communicate with others on paper. You must learn how to compose paragraphs so that the sequence of thoughts flows smoothly, easily, and logically from sentence to sentence. You must provide those bridges or links that will enable the reader to pass from sentence to sentence without being puzzled about the relationship of what is said in one sentence to what is said in the next sentence.

51

52 Development

Paragraphs should be adequately developed.

Generally, one- and two-sentence paragraphs are not justifiable, except for purposes of emphasis, transition, or dialogue.

Note that the previous sentence is also a paragraph, justifiable as such on the grounds that the writer wanted to give special emphasis to a principle by setting it aside in a paragraph by itself. Separate paragraphing for emphasis is a graphic device comparable to underlining a word or a phrase in a sentence for emphasis. Set aside in a paragraph by itself, an important idea achieves a prominence that would be missed if the idea were merged with other ideas in the same paragraph.

A one- or two-sentence paragraph can also be used to mark or signal a transition from one major division of a discourse to the next major division. These transitional paragraphs facilitate reading because they orient readers, reminding them of what has been discussed and alerting them to what is going to be discussed. Such paragraphs are like signposts marking the major stages of a journey. Note how the following two-sentence transitional paragraph looks backward to what has been discussed and forward to what will be discussed:

> After presenting his introduction to *Songs of Experience*, William Blake apparently feels that his readers have been sufficiently warned about their earthly predicament. Let us see now how he uses the poems in *Songs of Experience* to illustrate what the people might do to solve their problems.

52

One of the conventions of printing is that in representing dialogue in a story, we should begin a new paragraph every time the speaker changes. A paragraph of dialogue can be one sentence long or ten sentences long (any number of sentences, in fact). A paragraph of dialogue may also consist of only a phrase or a single word. Note the paragraphing of the following stretch of dialogue:

> "Look at that cloudless blue sky," Melvin said. "There doesn't seem to be any bottom to that blue. It's beautiful, isn't it?"
>
> "Yup," Hank muttered.
> "Remember yesterday?"
> "Yup."
> "I thought it would never stop raining."
> "Me too."

Once an exchange like that gets going, the author can dispense with the identifying tags, because each separate paragraph will mark the shift in speaker.

But except for the purposes of emphasis, transition, or dialogue, a one- or two-sentence paragraph can rarely be justified. One sentence is hardly enough to qualify as both the topic sentence and the development of the idea posed by that topic sentence. Many times even three- and four-sentence paragraphs are not adequately developed. You will frequently see one-, two-, and sometimes three-sentence paragraphs in a newspaper, but newspapers arbitrarily break up paragraphs into small units merely to facilitate reading. In the narrow columns of a newspaper, a five- or six-sentence paragraph would look forbiddingly dense. So the short paragraph is a convention used by all newspapers.

Judgment about whether a paragraph is adequately developed is, of course, a relative matter. Because some ideas need more development than others, no one can say, in the abstract, how many sentences a paragraph needs in order to be adequately developed. Each paragraph must be judged on its own terms and in the context in which it appears. If a paragraph has a topic sentence, for instance, that sentence can dictate how long the paragraph needs to be. What was done in the previous paragraph and what will be done in the paragraph that follows may dictate how long the middle paragraph needs to be.

Three samples of inadequately developed paragraphs will be displayed, and after each paragraph has been discussed, it will be presented in a revised version:

1. Corporations make frequent use of group conversation in order to develop communication among their employees. The effectiveness of this technique is one of the keys to successful communication between management and workers.

52

This sample paragraph and the two that follow have all been taken out of context, but even so, we can sense the inadequate development of these skimpy paragraphs. Paragraph **1**, for instance, raises some expectations that are not satisfied. The first sentence mentions that some corporations make frequent use of group conversation as a means of developing communication among their employees. If what preceded this paragraph did not define what "group conversation" is, we would expect this paragraph to give us that explanation. If the previous paragraph did define "group conversation," the first sentence of this paragraph would lead us to expect that some evidence or examples be given of the use of group conversations by corporations or some discussion of how the group conversations develop communication among the employees. Instead, the second sentence of paragraph **1** raises another set of expectations for readers: show us how this technique proves to be the key to successful communication between management and workers. The writer of this paragraph has to decide what the topic of the paragraph will be and then must develop that topic sufficiently in the rest of the paragraph.

Here is one way to adequately develop paragraph **1**:

1. The effectiveness of group conversation is one of the keys to successful communication between management and workers in many corporations. It is not sufficient that the opportunity for group conversation be set up. Those who conduct such sessions must make sure that everyone in the group makes a contribution to the conversation. And workers must not be intimidated by managers. Managers, for their part, must be willing to tolerate disagreement with their views from the workers. The greater the liveliness and the heatedness of the conversation, the greater chance that a favorable climate for real communication will be established. Genuine communication among the employees enhances amity and productivity. (*expanded by showing how group conversation fosters communication*)

Here is the second example of a thinly developed paragraph:

2. The young people now growing up in this drug-oriented atmosphere should be made aware of the disadvantages of their indulging in drugs, just as the young people of the previous generation were cautioned about the disadvantages of their engaging in premarital sex. In both cases, responsibility for one's actions is the chief lesson to be taught.

Even if paragraph **2** were a summary paragraph that followed a paragraph (or several paragraphs) in which the writer had discussed the disadvantages of indulging in drugs, the reader could reasonably expect the writer to say something more about the notion presented in the second sentence of this paragraph. What kind of legal or moral responsibilities do drug-users have to themselves? What kind of responsibilities do they have to their family and to society in general? Once they have been "hooked," can they still be held responsible for their actions? These questions suggest ways in which the writer might have expanded the thinly developed paragraph.

Here is one way in which that thinly developed paragraph might have been expanded:

2. Young people who indulge in drugs should be made aware of their responsibilities for their actions. They must be taught that an insatiable appetite for drugs has consequences not only for themselves but also for family, friends, and society. Parents are the ones who are hurt the most by a son or daughter who gets hooked on drugs. Parents suffer deeply when they see someone they love become a slave to drugs; and they also feel ashamed and guilt-ridden for their child's addiction. Friends, too, suffer anguish and humiliation; but they suffer most from the loss of the companionship of a former friend. The effects on society are too numerous to specify completely, but they include the dangers from an addict's resorting to violent crimes, the cost of maintaining special police forces, and the loss of a valuable contributing member of the community. Drug-users don't just run the risk of ruining their own lives; they can affect the lives of dozens of other people.
   (*expanded by pointing out the effects or consequences of a situation*)

Here is the third example of an inadequately developed paragraph:

3. Before we seek answers to those questions, however, we should settle on a definition of the term *illiteracy*. For most people, *illiteracy* signifies the inability to read and write.

A reader may feel that paragraph **3** is developed as much as it needs to be. The writer has suggested the need for a definition of the term **illiteracy** and in the next sentence has provided a definition of the term. But even lacking the context of both the paragraph that went before and the paragraph that came after this one, we can judge this paragraph to be inadequately developed. The mere

52

fact that the writer felt the need to seek a definition of a principal term before going on with the discussion indicates that the writer recognized the slipperiness of the term. The phrase that begins the second sentence, **For most people**, suggests that regardless of the common meaning of **illiteracy** (an inability to read and write), the term has other meanings for other people. What the reader expects to get in this paragraph and does not get is an exposition of the word's complex meanings. Refining the definition of the word **illiteracy** is one of the ways of expanding the paragraph:

3. Before we seek answers to those questions, however, we should settle on a definition of the term *illiteracy*. For most people, *illiteracy* signifies a person's inability to read and write. But that general definition does not reveal the wide range of disabilities covered by the term. There are those who cannot read or write anything in their native language. Others can read minimally, but they cannot write anything—not even their own names. A large number of people have minimal skills in reading and writing, but they cannot apply those skills to some of the ordinary tasks of day-to-day living—e.g., they cannot make sense of the written instructions on a can of weed-killer or fill out an application form. Such people are sometimes referred to as being "functionally illiterate." So whenever we discuss the problem of illiteracy with others, we should make sure what degree of disability people have in mind when they use the term *illiteracy*.

(*expanded by defining or explaining a key term*)

The first step in developing a paragraph is to consider its central idea—whether that is expressed in a topic sentence or merely implied—and determine what that idea commits you to do. It sometimes helps to ask yourself questions like those that were asked above about the second sample paragraph. If such questioning establishes what you are committed to do in a paragraph, you can then make a choice of the appropriate means of developing the paragraph. Here is a list of the common ways in which writers develop their paragraphs:

(a) They present examples or illustrations of what they are discussing.

(b) They cite data—facts, statistics, evidence, details, precedents—that corroborate or confirm what they are discussing.

(c) They quote, paraphrase, or summarize the testimony of others about what they are discussing.

(d) They relate an anecdote or event that has some bearing on what they are discussing.

(e) They define terms connected with what they are discussing.

(f) They compare or contrast what they are discussing with something else—usually something familiar to the readers.

(g) They explore the causes or reasons for the phenomenon or situation they are discussing.

(h) They point out the effects or consequences of the phenomenon or situation they are discussing.

(i) They explain how something operates.

(j) They describe the person, place, or thing they are discussing.

52

In the revisions of the examples of inadequately developed paragraphs, we have seen how one or more of these means of development was used to expand the paragraphs. If we inspect other well-developed paragraphs, we will find that these, and maybe other, means of development were used to flesh out the paragraphs.

PUNCTUATION

Graphic punctuation, which is the only kind dealt with in this section, is a feature of the written language exclusively. For the written language, it performs the kinds of function that intonation (pitch, stress, pause, and juncture) performs for the spoken language. Punctuation and intonation can be considered as part of the grammar of a language because they join with other grammatical devices (word order, inflections, and function words) to help convey meaning. If writers would regard punctuation as an integral—and often indispensable—part of the expressive system of a language, they might cease to think of it as just another nuisance imposed on them by editors and English teachers.

In *Structural Essentials of English* (New York: Harcourt Brace Jovanovich, 1956), Harold Whitehall has neatly summarized the four main functions of graphic punctuation:

- **For LINKING parts of sentences and words.**

  semicolon ;
  colon :
  dash —
  hyphen (for words only) -

● **For SEPARATING sentences and parts of sentences.**

period .
question mark ?
exclamation point !
comma ,

● **For ENCLOSING parts of sentences.**

pair of commas , . . . ,
pair of dashes — . . . —
pair of parentheses (. . .)
pair of brackets [. . .]
pair of quotation marks " . . . "

● **For INDICATING omissions.**

apostrophe (e.g., **don't, we'll, it's, we've**)
period (e.g., abbreviations, **Mrs., U.S., A. H. Robinson**)
dash (e.g., **John R——, D——n!**)
triple periods (. . . to indicate omitted words in a quotation)

Punctuation is strictly a convention. There is no reason in the nature of things why the mark **?** should be used in English to indicate a question. The Greek language, for instance, uses **;** (what we call a semicolon) to mark questions. Nor is there any reason in the nature of things why the single comma should be a separating device rather than a linking device. It is usage that has established the distinctive functions of the various marks of punctuation. And although styles of punctuation have changed somewhat from century to century and even from country to country, the conventions of punctuation set forth in the following section are the current conventions in the United States. Although publishers of newspapers, magazines, and books often have style manuals that prescribe, for their own editors and writers, a style of punctuation that may differ in some particulars from the prevailing conventions, writers who observe the conventions of punctuation set forth in this section can rest assured that they are following the predominant system in the United States.

60   Comma, Compound Sentence

Put a comma in front of the coordinating conjunction that joins the independent clauses of a compound sentence.

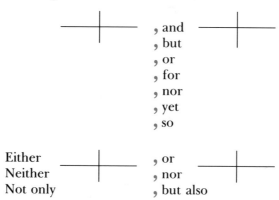

60

Examples of compound sentences that need a comma:

1. The purpose of the letter is evident and the organization of the letter is excellent.

rewrite:

The purpose of the letter is evident, and the organization of the letter is excellent.

2. Ice was forming on the wings and a strong wind was blowing us off course but no one panicked.

rewrite:
   Ice was forming on the wings, and a strong wind was blowing us off course, but no one panicked.

3. Johann Strauss composed hundreds of dances over the years but his art remained fresh and young.

rewrite:
   Johann Strauss composed hundreds of dances over the years, but his art remained fresh and young.

4. They resented this kind of treatment yet they agreed to sign the contract.

rewrite:
   They resented this kind of treatment, yet they agreed to sign the contract.

5. He returned the book for his mother refused to pay any more fines.

rewrite:
   He returned the book, for his mother refused to pay any more fines.

60

6. Either the President will veto the bill or the Supreme Court will rule that the bill is unconstitutional.

rewrite:
   Either the President will veto the bill, or the Supreme Court will rule that the bill is unconstitutional.

This convention of the comma comes into play only in compound sentences (sentences composed of two or more independent clauses) or in compound-complex sentences (sentences composed of two or more independent clauses and at least one dependent clause). According to **62** in this section, pairs of words, phrases, or clauses (except independent clauses) joined by one of the coordinating conjunctions should *not* be separated with a comma.

This practice of using a comma probably developed because in many compound sentences, the absence of the comma could lead to an initial misreading of the sentence. In sentence 5, for instance, it would be quite natural for us to read **for** as a preposition and consequently to read the sentence this way:

He returned the book for his mother. . .

But when we came to the verb **refused**, we would realize that we had misread the sentence, and we would have to go back and reread it.

Some handbooks authorize you to omit this separating comma under certain conditions. However, if you *invariably* insert a comma before the coordinating conjunction that joins the independent clauses, you never have to pause to consider whether these conditions are present, and you can be confident that your sentence will always be read correctly the first time. So the safest practice is *always* to insert the comma before the coordinating conjunction or before the second of the correlative conjunctions (**either . . . or**; **neither . . . nor**; **not only . . . but also**) that join the main clauses of a compound or a compound-complex sentence.

61 Comma, Introductory

Introductory words, phrases, or clauses should be separated from the main (independent) clause by a comma.

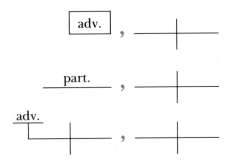

Examples of introductory words, phrases, and clauses that need a comma:

61

1. Before the executives depended on a committee of engineers to advise them.

rewrite:
   Before, the executives depended on a committee of engineers to advise them.

2. In both positions I have recommended that employees be adequately insured before they are permitted to undertake the job.

rewrite:
   In both positions, I have recommended that employees be adequately insured before they are permitted to undertake the job.

3. Although she vehemently protested the violence was not as destructive as she predicted it would be.

rewrite:
> Although she vehemently protested, the violence was not as destructive as she predicted it would be.

4. Not having seen the light at the intersection I failed to stop.
rewrite:
> Not having seen the light at the intersection, I failed to stop.

5. Inside his office looked like a bordello.
rewrite:
> Inside, his office looked like a bordello.

The reason for the comma after introductory elements is that the comma facilitates the reading of the sentence and often prevents an initial misreading of it. Without the "protective" comma, the syntax of the five sample sentence structures above would probably be initially misread. Readers would probably read the sample sentences this way the first time:

1. Before the executives depended on a committee. . .

2. In both positions [that] I have recommended. . .

3. Although she vehemently protested the violence. . .

4. Not having seen the light at the intersection I failed. . .

5. Inside his office. . .

The insertion of a comma after each of these introductory elements would have prevented even the possibility of that kind of misreading.

Even in those instances where there is little or no chance of an initial misreading, however, the insertion of a comma after the introductory word, phrase, or clause will facilitate the reading of the sentence. If you read the following sentences twice, the first time without a comma, the second time with a comma after the introductory word, phrase, or clause, you will discover that it is easier to read and understand the sentences that have a comma after the introductory element:

> Besides the crowd was not impressed by his flaming oratory.

> Having failed to impress the crowd with his flaming oratory he tried another tactic.

> After he saw that his flaming oratory had not impressed the crowd he tried another tactic.

If you *always* insert a comma after an introductory word, phrase, or clause, you will not have to consider each time whether it would be safe to omit the comma, and you can be confident that your sentence will not be misread.

62 No Comma, Coordinating Conjunction

Pairs of words, phrases, or dependent clauses joined by one of the coordinating conjunctions should not be separated with a comma.

62

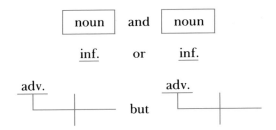

Examples of pairs incorrectly separated by a comma:

1. These theoretical computations do not take into consideration wind speed, or temperature variations.
    (*two noun phrases joined by* **or**)

rewrite:

These theoretical computations do not take into consideration wind speed or temperature variations.

2. The response of the language experts to these changes is skeptical, and even predictable.
(*two adjectives joined by* **and**)

rewrite:

The response of the language experts to these changes is skeptical and even predictable.

3. Most of the students are not equally prepared for higher education, and don't fit into the "box" of expectations established by the Admissions Office.
(*two verb phrases joined by* **and**)

rewrite:

Most of the students are not equally prepared for higher education and don't fit into the "box" of expectations established by the Admissions Office.

4. We knew that the play would be dull, and that we would have to stand in line to get seats.
(*two noun clauses joined by* **and**)

rewrite:

We knew that the play would be dull and that we would have to stand in line to get seats.

The principle behind this convention is that what has been joined by one means (the coordinating conjunction) should not then be separated by another means (the comma, a separating device). The function of the coordinating conjunction is to join units of equal rank (e.g., nouns with nouns, verbs with verbs, prepositional phrases with prepositional phrases, adjective clauses with adjective clauses). Once pairs of coordinate units have been joined by the conjunction, it makes no sense to separate them with a comma—as has been done in all the sample sentences above.

A pair of *independent* clauses does not come under this rule. According to **60**, a comma should be inserted before the coordinating conjunction, because in this structure, the omission of the comma could lead—and often does lead— to an initial misreading of the sentence. But there are almost no instances where the use of a comma would help the reading of pairs of words, phrases, or dependent clauses joined by a coordinating conjunction. As a matter of fact, sentence **4** is harder to read because of the comma that separates the two noun clauses. The comma in that sentence only confuses the reader.

An exception to this convention occurs in the case of suspended structures, as in the following sentences:

> The report about the biologist's struggle with, and triumph over, numerous obstacles fascinated me.

> We must never relinquish our interest in, or our respect for, the accomplishments of our ancestors.

The phrases **struggle with** and **triumph over** are called *suspended structures* because they are left "hanging" until they are completed by the noun phrase **numerous obstacles**. Likewise, the phrases **interest in** and **respect for** are "suspended" until they are completed by the phrase **the accomplishments of our ancestors**.

62

Another exception to this convention occurs in the structure where the word or phrase following the first word or phrase presents not an alternative to the previous word or phrase (as in "right or wrong" and "apples or oranges") but an *explanatory appositive* for the previous word or phrase. In such cases, the explanatory appositive is enclosed with a pair of commas, as in the following examples:

> Her fealty, or devotion, never wavered.

> The holograph, or handwritten manuscript, was carefully examined by archaeologists.

With these two exceptions, the joining device (the conjunction) and the separating device (the comma) should not work against one another.

63 Comma, Series

Use a comma to separate a series of coordinate words, phrases, or clauses.

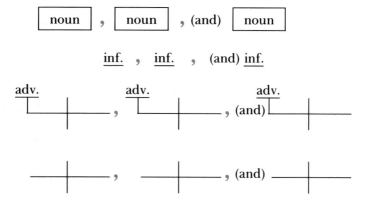

*(The parentheses around **and** in the diagrams indicate that the coordinating conjunction between the last two members of a series may sometimes be dispensed with. For instance, the phrasing **The tall, robust, gray-haired soldier rose to speak** is stylistically preferable to **The tall, robust, and gray-haired soldier rose to speak**.)*

Examples of series lacking one or more commas:

1. Some of the tactics they have adopted for dealing with parking problems include arriving very early, incessantly circling the

parking lot, parking on nearby streets and even changing their residence so that they can walk to work.
(*a series of gerund phrases*)

rewrite:

Some of the tactics they have adopted for dealing with parking problems include arriving very early, incessantly circling the parking lot, parking on nearby streets, and even changing their residence so that they can walk to work.

2. She announced that she was staying in bed that she was not cooking lunch for anybody and that she would decide later about dinner.
(*a series of noun clauses*)

rewrite:

She announced that she was staying in bed, that she was not cooking lunch for anybody, and that she would decide later about dinner.

3. Four techniques commonly used in the sciences are analysis, classification, definition and description.
(*a series of nouns*)

rewrite:

Four techniques commonly used in the sciences are analysis, classification, definition, and description.

4. Our task is to arrest the pollution, alleviate the discomfort of the inhabitants and discover the cause of the contamination.
(*a series of verb phrases*)

rewrite:

Our task is to arrest the pollution, alleviate the discomfort of the inhabitants, and discover the cause of the contamination.

63

Whereas the convention stated in **62** says that *pairs* of coordinate words, phrases, or clauses should not be separated by a comma, the convention governing a *series* of coordinate words, phrases, and clauses says that these units should be separated by commas. (*A series is to be understood as a sequence of three or more coordinate units.*) Built on the principle of parallelism (see **27**), the series always involves words, phrases, or clauses of a similar kind. So a series should never couple dissimilar grammatical elements—for example, nouns with adjectives, prepositional phrases with infinitive phrases, adjective clauses with adverb clauses.

The convention that is recommended here follows this formula:

a, b, and c

Another acceptable formula for the series is

a, b and c

where no comma is used between the last two members of the series when they are joined by a coordinating conjunction. The formula **a, b, and c** is adopted here because the alternative formula (**a, b and c**) sometimes leads to ambiguity. Consider the following example, which used the **a, b and c** formula:

> Please send me a gross each of the red, green, blue, orange and black ties.

63

The shipping clerk who received that order might wonder whether five gross of ties (**red, green, blue, orange, black**) were being ordered or if only four groups (**red, green, blue, orange-and-black**) were being ordered. If five gross were being ordered, a comma after **orange** would clarify the order; if four gross were being ordered, hyphens should have been used to signify the combination of colors.

A more common instance of the ambiguity that is sometimes created by the use of the **a, b and c** formula is the following:

> He appealed to the management, the presidents and the vice-presidents.

In this sentence, it is not clear whether he appealed to three different groups (**management, presidents, vice-presidents**)—a meaning that would have been clearly indicated by the **a, b, and c** formula—or to only one group,

management, who are then specified in two appositives, **presidents** and **vice-presidents**.

Since there is never any chance of ambiguity if you invariably use the **a, b, and c** formula, you would be well advised to adopt this option for punctuating a series.

64 Comma, Nonrestrictive

Nonrestrictive adjective clauses should be enclosed with a pair of commas.

Examples of nonrestrictive adjective clauses that should be enclosed with commas:

64

1. Elmer who had dropped the spider down my neck was looking nonchalantly at the ceiling.

rewrite:

Elmer, who had dropped the spider down my neck, was looking nonchalantly at the ceiling.

2. This same book cites other *r* problems which include *quintruplets* for *quintuplets* and *surpress* for *suppress*.

rewrite:

This same book cites other *r* problems, which include *quintruplets* for *quintuplets* and *surpress* for *suppress*.

3. His oldest brother who is a physicist is the Chief of Staff at Rockwell International.

rewrite:

His oldest brother, who is a physicist, is the Chief of Staff at Rockwell International.

4. This plant deals only with rural stores which normally are closed during the winter months.

rewrite:

This plant deals only with rural stores, which normally are closed during the winter months.

A nonrestrictive adjective clause is one that supplies information about the noun that it modifies but information that is not needed to identify or specify the particular person, place, or thing that is being talked about. (The four **that** clauses in the previous sentence, for instance, are *restrictive* adjective clauses—clauses that supply *necessary* identifying or specifying information about the nouns that they modify.)

In sentence **2**, the adjective clause **who had dropped the spider down my neck** supplies additional information about **Elmer**, but this information is not needed to identify the mischievous person, because that person is sufficiently identified by his proper name **Elmer**.

One test to determine whether an adjective clause is nonrestrictive is to read the sentence without the adjective clause, and if the particular person, place, or thing being talked about is sufficiently identified by what is left, the clause can be considered nonrestrictive—and, according to the convention, should be marked off with commas. If, for instance, you were to drop the adjective clause from sentence **3** and say **His oldest brother is the Chief of Staff at Rockwell International**, your readers would not have to ask, "Which one of your brothers is the Chief of Staff at Rockwell International?" That brother is adequately specified by the adjective **oldest**, since there can be only one **oldest** brother. The adjective clause **who is a physicist** merely supplied some additional but nonessential information about the oldest brother.

Another test to determine whether an adjective clause is

nonrestrictive is the *intonation* test. Read these two written versions of sentence 4 aloud:

> This plant deals only with rural stores which are normally closed during the winter months.

> This plant deals only with rural stores, which are normally closed during the winter months.

In reading the second version aloud, speakers of the language would pause briefly after the word **stores** (that is, in the place where the comma is) and would lower the pitch of their voices slightly in enunciating the clause **which are normally closed during the winter months**. In reading the first version, however, speakers would read right through without a pause and would not lower the pitch of their voices in reading the adjective clause.

In writing, it makes a *significant* difference whether the adjective clause in a sentence is marked off with commas or not. *With* the comma, sentence 4 means that the plant deals exclusively with rural stores (which, incidentally, are usually closed during the winter months). *Without* the comma, sentence 4 means that the plant deals exclusively with rural stores that are closed during the winter months (in other words, the plant does not deal at all with those rural stores that are *open* during the winter months). Those two meanings are quite different from each other, and for that reason, it is extremely important, in a written text, whether or not the adjective clause is marked off with commas.

There are some instances in which the adjective clause is almost invariably nonrestrictive:

(a) Where the antecedent is a **proper noun**, the adjective clause is usually nonrestrictive:

> New York City, which has the largest urban population in the United States, . . .

> The College of William and Mary, which was founded in the year 1693, . . .

64

(b) Where, in the nature of things, there could be **only one such** person, place, or thing, the adjective clause is usually nonrestrictive:

> My mother, who is now forty-six years old, . . .
>
> His fingerprints, which are on file in Washington, . . .

(c) Where the identity of the antecedent has been clearly established by the **previous context**, the adjective clause is usually nonrestrictive:

> The plant, which is now 84 years old, . . . (where the previous sentence has identified the particular plant being talked about)
>
> Such revolutions, which never enlist the sympathies of the majority of the people, . . . (where the kinds of revolutions being talked about have been specified in the previous sentences or paragraphs)

Which is the usual relative pronoun that introduces nonrestrictive clauses referring to non-human antecedents; **that** is the more common relative pronoun in restrictive adjective clauses referring to such antecedents. **Who** (or its inflected forms **whose** and **whom**) is the usual relative pronoun when the antecedent is a person; **that**, however, may also be used when the antecedent is a person and the clause is restrictive: either "the men whom I admire" or "the men that I admire."

65 No Comma, Restrictive

Restrictive adjective clauses should not be marked off with a pair of commas.

Examples of adjective clauses that should not be marked off with a pair of commas:

1. All children, who were in the front row, received free ice cream.

rewrite:
   All children who were in the front row received free ice cream.

2. This information should include a map, that specifies the areas where it is permissible to park.

rewrite:
   This information should include a map that specifies the areas where it is permissible to park.

3. Middle-aged operators, who have slow reflexes, should not handle high-speed machinery.

rewrite:
   Middle-aged operators who have slow reflexes should not handle high-speed machinery.

4. All streets, alleys, and thoroughfares, which are in the public domain, should be maintained by the city.

rewrite:
   All streets, alleys, and thoroughfares that are in the public domain should be maintained by the city.

65

A restrictive adjective clause is one that identifies or specifies the particular person, place, or thing being talked about. It "restricts" the noun that it modifies; it "defines"—that is, "draws boundaries around"—the noun being talked about. Nonrestrictive clauses, as we saw in **64**, give *additional* information about the nouns that they modify, but they do not serve to *identify* or *specify* the nouns that they modify.

In sentence **1**, the adjective clause **who were in the first row** is restrictive because it identifies, defines, designates, specifies *which* children received free ice cream. The writer of that sentence did not intend to say that *all* children received free ice cream, but with the commas enclosing that adjective clause, the sentence does suggest that all of them did receive free ice cream. The writer of this sentence meant to say that only all of the children in the first row received free ice cream. Leaving out the enclosing commas will make the sentence say what the writer intended to say.

If the commas in sentences **2**, **3**, and **4** are omitted, the sentences will say what the writers intended to say.

According to the convention, nonrestrictive clauses modifying nonhuman nouns should be introduced with the relative pronoun **which**, and restrictive adjective clauses modifying nonhuman nouns should be introduced with the relative pronoun **that**:

> Governments, which are instituted to protect human rights, should be responsive to the will of the people. (*nonrestrictive*)

> Governments that want to remain in favor with their constituents must be responsive to the will of the people. (*restrictive*)

65

Accordingly, in revising sentence **4**, we changed from the nonrestrictive pronoun **which** to the restrictive pronoun **that**: All streets, alleys, and thoroughfares **that** are in the public domain should be maintained by the city.

Here is another distinctive fact about the phrasing of restrictive and nonrestrictive clauses: the relative pronoun may sometimes be omitted in restrictive clauses, but it may never be omitted in nonrestrictive clauses. Note that it is impossible in English to drop the relative pronouns **who** and **whom** from the following nonrestrictive clauses:

> Kwong Bruce, who is our best engineer, will not cooperate with me.

> John, whom I respect a great deal, hardly speaks to me.

(In the first sentence, however, the clause **who is our best engineer** could be reduced to an appositive phrase: **Kwong Bruce,** *our best engineer,* **will not cooperate with me.**)

In restrictive adjective clauses, we sometimes have the option of using or not using the relative pronoun:

The one whom I respect a great deal hardly notices me. (*with the relative pronoun*)

The one that I respect a great deal hardly notices me. (*with the relative pronoun*)

The one I respect a great deal hardly notices me. (*without the relative pronoun*)

In restrictive adjective clauses like these, where the relative pronoun serves as the object of the verb of the adjective clause, the relative pronoun may be omitted. The relative pronoun in restrictive clauses may also be omitted if it serves as the object of a preposition in the adjective clause: "The chemist I gave the formula to disappeared" (here the understood *whom* or *that* serves as the object of the preposition **to**). However, the relative pronoun may *not* be omitted when it serves as the subject of the restrictive adjective clause:

He who exalts himself shall be humbled.
(**who** *cannot be omitted here*)

The money that was set aside for scholarships was squandered on roads.
(**that** *cannot be omitted here*)

You should learn the difference between restrictive and nonrestrictive clauses because the meaning of a sentence can change radically if commas are put in where they should not be or if they are omitted where they should be.

65

66 Semicolon, Compound Sentence

If the independent clauses of a compound sentence are not joined by one of the coordinating conjunctions, they should be joined by a semicolon.

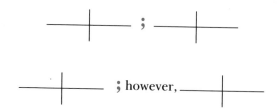

Examples of compound sentences that should be joined by a semicolon:

66

1. These findings are based on empirical research, however, we must not forget that important discoveries have also been made by deductive reasoning.

rewrite:

These findings are based on empirical research; however, we must not forget that important discoveries have also been made by deductive reasoning.

2. All the students spontaneously supported the team, they wanted to show their loyalty, even though they were disappointed with the outcome of the game.

rewrite:

All the students spontaneously supported the team; they wanted to show their loyalty, even though they were disappointed with the outcome of the game.

3. We maintained a computerized storage system for two years, later we established a highly sophisticated retrieval system.

rewrite:
> We maintained a computerized storage system for two years; later we established a highly sophisticated retrieval system.

4. To arrest this expensive loss of heat, you should insulate your house, in fact, it would be advisable for you to install this insulation as soon as possible.

rewrite:
> To arrest this expensive loss of heat, you should insulate your house; in fact, it would be advisable for you to install this insulation as soon as possible.

As pointed out in section **60**, the coordinating conjunctions are **and**, **but**, **or**, **for**, **nor**, **yet**, **so**. In the absence of one of those words, the independent clauses of a compound sentence should be spliced together with a punctuation device: the semicolon.

Words and phrases such as **however**, **therefore**, **then**, **indeed**, **moreover**, **thus**, **nevertheless**, **consequently**, **furthermore**, **in fact**, **on the other hand**, **on the contrary** are not coordinating conjunctions; they are called *conjunctive adverbs*. Conjunctive adverbs provide logical links between sentences and between parts of sentences, but they do not function as grammatical splicers. Unlike coordinating conjunctions, which must always be placed *between* the two elements they join, conjunctive adverbs enjoy some freedom of movement in the sentence.

66

In sentence **1**, the word **however** is placed between the two independent clauses, but evidence that this conjunctive adverb is not serving as the grammatical splicer of the two clauses is provided by the fact that **however** can be shifted to another position in the sentence: **These findings are based on empirical research; we must not forget, however, that important discoveries have also been made by deductive reasoning.** The coordinating conjunction **but**, on the other hand, which is equivalent to **however**, could occupy no other position in the sentence than *between* the end of the first clause (after the word **research**) and the beginning of the next clause (before the word **we**).

Nor can the independent clauses of a compound sentence be joined by a comma, because the comma is a separating device, not a joining device. Compound sentences so punctuated—as is sentence **2**—are called **comma splices** (see **30**). As indicated in **60**, if a compound sentence is joined by one of the coordinating conjunctions, a comma should be put in front of the conjunction to mark off the end of one independent clause and the beginning of the next independent clause. But whenever a coordinating conjunction is not present to join the independent clauses, a semicolon must be used to join them. The semicolon serves both to mark the division between the two clauses and to join them.

Sometimes it is advisable to use both a semicolon and a coordinating conjunction to join the independent clauses of a compound sentence. When the clauses are unusually long and have commas within them, a semicolon placed before the coordinating conjunction helps to signal the end of one clause and the beginning of the next one, as in this example:

> Struggling to salvage what was left of the project, he pleaded with his supervisor, who was notoriously softhearted, to grant him an extension of time to complete his investigation, to draw his conclusions, and to make his report**; but** he forgot that, even with the best of intentions, he had only so many hours a day in which he could work productively.

Here the coordinating conjunction **but** serves to join the two main clauses of the compound sentence, but the use of the semicolon in addition to the conjunction makes it easier for us to read the sentence.

67 Semicolon, Independent Clauses

Whenever you use a semicolon, be sure that you have an independent clause on both sides of the semicolon.

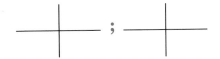

Examples of failure to observe this convention:

1. To illustrate how publication takes precedence over teaching; my history professor would not let me make up the examination I missed when I was in the hospital because he was "too busy" preparing his latest book to go to press.

rewrite:
   To illustrate how publication takes precedence over teaching, I cite the example of my history professor, who would not let me make up the examination I missed when I was in the hospital because he was "too busy" preparing his latest book to go to press.

2. She keeps us interested enough to go on reading; even though we don't always understand everything we read.

rewrite:
   She keeps us interested enough to go on reading, even though we don't always understand everything we read.

3. As shown in Figure 2, there were several irregular surges of voltage during the test; proving that the safety devices designed for this project had not yet been perfected.

rewrite:
   As shown in Figure 2, there were several irregular surges of voltage during the test; these irregular surges of voltage prove

67

that the safety devices designed for this project had not yet been perfected.

4. We will submit some information as soon as we discover it; other information being withheld because it is classified.

rewrite:

We will submit some information as soon as we discover it; other information is being withheld because it is classified.

This convention is the corollary of **66**. It cautions against using the semicolon to join elements of unequal rank. Accordingly, if there is an independent clause on one side of the semicolon, there must be a balancing independent clause on the other side of the semicolon.

In all of the examples above, a semicolon has been used to join units of *unequal* rank. In three of the sentences (**2**, **3**, **4**), there is an independent clause on the *left-hand* side of the semicolon; however, there is no independent clause on the *right-hand* side of the semicolon in any of those three sentences. What is on the right-hand side of the semicolon could be called a sentence fragment (see **29**).

In sentence **2**, there is an independent clause **She keeps us interested enough to go on reading** on the left-hand side of the semicolon, but on the right-hand side of the semicolon, there is only the adverb clause **even though we don't always understand everything we read**. That adverb clause belongs with, depends on, the first clause. Since it is an integral part of the first clause, that adverb clause should be *joined* with the independent clause. The effect of the semicolon is to make the adverb clause part of *another* clause that begins after the semicolon. But on the right-hand side of the semicolon, there is no independent clause that the subordinate, dependent adverb clause can be a part of. One way to correct the sentence is to supply an independent clause, on the right-hand side of the semi-colon, that the adverb clause can adhere to—e.g., **She**

67

keeps us interested enough to go on reading; she just wants us to go on reading, even though we don't always understand everything we read. But a simpler way to correct the original sentence is to substitute a comma for the semicolon, as we have done in our revision.

We corrected sentence **1** by substituting a comma for the semicolon after the word **teaching**. We have revised sentences **3** and **4**, however, by converting the string of words on the right-hand side of the semicolon into an independent clause, so that the semicolon is joining units of equal rank.

68 Colon for Lead-in

Use a colon after a grammatically complete lead-in sentence that formally announces a subsequent enumeration, specification, illustration, or extended quotation.

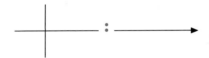

The following sentences either need a colon or use a colon improperly:

1. The survey revealed that the four most common terms for the practice of searching for a Saturday-night date are: *scope, scam, pick-up,* and *cruise.*

rewrite:
   The survey revealed that the four most common terms for the practice of searching for a Saturday-night date are these: *scope, scam, pick-up,* and *cruise. (an enumeration)*

2. I believe that this lack of confidence is attributable to at least two factors, (1) a reluctance on the part of the public to learn the rules of their native language, (2) an aversion to a change of the rules that results in a discrediting of Latin grammar.

rewrite:

I believe that this lack of confidence is attributable to at least two factors: (1) a reluctance on the part of the public to learn the rules of their native language, (2) an aversion to a change of the rules that results in a discrediting of Latin grammar. (*a specification*)

3. The reason given for the failure of the system was incontrovertible—the electrical-supply source was defective.

rewrite:

The reason given for the failure of the system was incontrovertible: the electrical-supply source was defective. (*an explanation*)

4. The sales representative has adopted this approach. After displaying his product and extolling its virtues, he asks the homemaker for a small rug that needs cleaning.

rewrite:

The sales representative has adopted this approach: after displaying his product and extolling its virtues, he asks the homemaker for a small rug that needs cleaning. (*an illustration*)

68

A colon signals that what *follows* it is a spelling out, a detailing of what was formally announced in the clause on the left-hand side of the colon. What differentiates the colon from the dash as a symbolic mark of punctuation is that the colon throws the reader's attention *forward*, whereas the dash as a linking device throws the reader's attention backward (see **69**). Although a word, phrase, clause or series of words, phrases, or clauses can follow the colon, there must be an independent clause (a grammatically complete sentence) on the left-hand side of the colon.

In accord with this principle, sentence 1 should not have been punctuated the way it was; that punctuation makes no more sense than punctuating a sentence this way:

My name is: John Adams.

In both cases, the words following the colon are needed to complete the sentence grammatically. So either the colon must be dropped altogether, or enough words must be added to make the clause on the left-hand side of the colon a grammatically complete sentence. In sentence 1, for instance, put **these** or **as follows** after the verb **are**.

In sentence 2, the comma after **two factors** should be replaced with a colon. Since the lead-in clause in sentence 3 throws the reader's attention forward to get the reason for the failure, the dash after **incontrovertible** should be replaced by a colon. In sentence 4, we should link the second sentence to the first sentence by substituting a colon for the period after the word **approach**.

A colon is conventionally used after the lead-in sentence that introduces an extended quotation. Here is an example of that use—a use that is common in research papers:

68

Professor Yoko Tomida has testified that the blips on the monitor do not necessarily indicate lunar emanations:

Many astronomers have labored under the false impression that the magnetic fields that have been recorded on their oscilloscopes represent emanations from the surface of the moon. But a series of recent experiments have conclusively discredited that traditional view. The current opinion is that these electronic blips on our screens were produced by electrical pulsations from black holes in that part of the galaxy. The findings of my studies support this opinion.

69 Dash for Summation

Use a dash when the word or word-group that follows it constitutes a summation, an amplification, or a reversal of what went before it.

Examples of sentences that need to be punctuated with a dash:

1. Statistics 502, Mathematics 421, Computer Graphics 542, and Economics 448, these are the courses that I regard as being pertinent to the job for which I am applying.

   rewrite:

   Statistics 502, Mathematics 421, Computer Graphics 542, and Economics 448—these are the courses that I regard as being pertinent to the job for which I am applying. (*a summation*)

2. If he was criticized, he would become sullen and tight-lipped, a reaction that did not endear him to his colleagues.

   rewrite:

   If he was criticized, he would become sullen and tight-lipped—a reaction that did not endear him to his colleagues. (*a commentary*)

3. The basic material is constructed of composite synthetics, a graphite fabric wrapped around a hollow rod made of nylon.

   rewrite:

   The basic material is constructed of composite synthetics—a graphite fabric wrapped around a hollow rod made of nylon. (*an amplification*)

4. She kneads the ball of clay, centers the clay on the potter's wheel, shapes the clay in the form of an urn, and then flattens the urn with a wooden mallet.

   rewrite:

   She kneads the ball of clay, centers the clay on the potter's wheel, shapes the clay in the form of an urn—and then flattens the urn with a wooden mallet. (*a reversal*)

Unlike the colon (see **68**), which directs the reader's attention *forward*, the dash usually directs the reader's attention *backward*. What follows the dash, when it is used as a linking device, looks back to what preceded it for the particulars or the details that spell out the meaning or invest the meaning with pungency or irony.

The colon and the dash are usually not interchangeable marks of punctuation. They signal a different relationship between the word-groups that precede them and those that follow them. After much practice in reading and writing, one develops a sense for the subtle distinction in relationships signaled by the punctuation in the following sentences:

> The reaction of the crowd signified only one thing: apathy.
>
> The people clearly indicated their indifference to the provocative speech—an apathy that later came back to haunt them.

In the first sentence, the lead-in clause before the colon clearly alerts the reader to expect a specification of what is hinted at in that lead-in clause. In the second sentence, there is no such alerting of the reader in the lead-in clause; but following the dash, there is an unexpected commentary on what was said in the lead-in clause, a summary commentary that forces the reader to look backward and that receives a special emphasis by being set off with a dash. The colon and the dash are both linking devices, but they signal different kinds of thought relationships between the parts of the sentence. Frequently, the dash signals a less formal relationship than the colon does.

69

70 Dash, Parenthetical Elements

Use a pair of dashes to enclose abrupt parenthetical elements that occur within a sentence.

— . . . —

Examples of parenthetical elements that should be enclosed with a pair of dashes:

1. I learned from this situation, and so will you, that if something sounds totally illogical to you, it probably is.

rewrite:

I learned from this situation—and so will you—that if something sounds totally illogical to you, it probably is.

2. One of them (let me call him Jim Prude) is clean-shaven and dresses like an Ivy Leaguer of the late 1950s.

rewrite:

One of them—let me call him Jim Prude—is clean-shaven and dresses like an Ivy Leaguer of the late 1950s.

3. The research team faced the difficulty, or should I say the impossibility, of controlling the temperatures to which the shrubs were exposed.

rewrite:

The research team faced the difficulty—or should I say the impossibility?—of controlling the temperatures to which the shrubs were exposed.

4. For many doctors, the risk of a misdiagnosis, and a lawsuit for malpractice, has influenced them to order an extensive series of costly medical tests.

rewrite:

For many doctors, the risk of a misdiagnosis—and a lawsuit for malpractice—has influenced them to order an extensive series of costly medical tests.

70

The three devices used to set off parenthetical elements in written prose are commas, parentheses, and dashes. The kind of parenthetical element that should be enclosed with a pair of dashes is the kind that interrupts the normal syntactical flow of the sentence. What characterizes all of the parenthetical elements in the examples above is that they abruptly arrest the normal flow of the sentence to add some qualifying or rectifying comment. The rhetorical effect of the enclosing dashes is to alert the reader to the interruption and thereby to help the reader understand the sentence.

A pair of parentheses is another typographical device used to mark off parenthetical elements in a sentence. Enclosure within parentheses is used mainly for those elements that merely add information or identification, as in sentences like these:

> All the companies that used the service were charged a small fee (usually $500) and were required to sign a contract (an "exclusive-use" agreement).

> The manager of each franchise is expected to report monthly to NARM (National Association of Retail Merchants) and to "rotate" (take turns doing various jobs) every two weeks.

70

The typographical device used to set off the mildest kind of interrupting element is a pair of commas. Whether to enclose a parenthetical element with commas, parentheses, or dashes is often more a matter of stylistic choice than a matter of grammatical necessity. There are degrees of interruption and emphasis, and with practice, a writer develops an instinct for knowing when to mark off parenthetical elements with commas (lowest degree of interruption and emphasis), when to mark them off with parentheses (middle degree), and when to mark them off with dashes (highest degree). Consider the degrees of interruption and emphasis in the following sentences:

That agency, as we have since learned, reported the incident directly to the Department of Justice.

During the postwar years (at least from 1946 to 1952), no one in the agency dared challenge a directive from higher up.

When the order was challenged, the attorney general—some claim it was his wife—put through a call to the President.

After much practice in writing, you will eventually learn how to detect the differences in degree of interruption and emphasis—and, consequently, to use the appropriate punctuation marks.

71 Formation of Dash

A dash is made on the typewriter with two unspaced hyphens and with no space before the dash or after the dash. (In handwriting, the dash should be made slightly longer than a hyphen.)

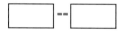

Because a typewriter or a word processor does not have a separate key for a dash, you have to make a dash with two hyphens. Do not hit the spacebar *before* the first hyphen, *between* the first and second hyphen, or *after* the second hyphen. In short, do not hit the spacebar at all in forming the dash on the typewriter or on the word processor. When you are handwriting a text, you have to distinguish a dash from a hyphen by making the dash slightly longer than the hyphen.

Here is an illustration of the proper way to form the dash on the typewriter or on the word processor:

```
She forgot——if she ever knew——the functions of

the various marks of punctuation.
```

Here are some incorrect ways of forming the dash on a typewriter or on a word processor.

```
forgot-if          forgot – if

forgot —— if       forgot – – if
```

71

MECHANICS

The graphic devices dealt with in this section might be, and often are, classified as punctuation. But because such graphic devices as italics, capitalization, and numbers are not correlated—as punctuation marks are—with the intonational patterns of the spoken language, these devices are grouped in a separate section under the heading Mechanics. In the spoken language, a word printed with an initial capital letter is pronounced no differently from the same word printed with an initial lowercase letter. Nor is the italicized title of a book pronounced any differently from that same title printed without italics. (Italics used for emphasizing a word or phrase, however, do correspond to stress in the spoken language.) Even quotation marks, which we might regard as correlated with the spoken language, do not correspond to anything the voice does when it quotes direct speech.

But whether we classify these graphic devices as punctuation or as mechanics is immaterial. What is important to remember is that these devices are part of the written language exclusively and that they facilitate the reading of that language. Most readers would have at least momentary difficulty making sense of the following string of words:

> Jill cried buckets as many as you can fetch Jack thought I don't have to please you over there she continued nuts pails they're called yelled Jack

If the proper punctuation and mechanics were used with that string of words, readers would be spared the momentary difficulty:

> Jill cried, "Buckets! As many as you can fetch!" Jack thought, "I don't have to!" "Please, you over there!" she continued. "Nuts! *Pails* they're called!" yelled Jack.

Deprived of the resources that the human voice possesses to clarify the meaning of words as spoken, you should be eager to see all those typographical devices that make it easier for your readers to grasp what you are trying to convey.

80 Quotation Marks with Period and Comma

The period or the comma always goes inside the closing quotation mark.

,"   ."

Examples of sentences with misplaced quotation marks:

80

1. Anxious to find out my class schedule for the Autumn Quarter, I ripped open the envelope and discovered the chilling notation "Closed out".

rewrite:
> Anxious to find out my class schedule for the Autumn Quarter, I ripped open the envelope and discovered the chilling notation "Closed out."

2. "Good morning, Mr. Simmons", she said.

rewrite:
> "Good morning, Mr. Simmons," she said.

3. In his *Philosophical Grammar*, Noah Webster pays homage to

national usage by accepting *you was* because "national usage determines correctness in grammar".

rewrite:

In his *Philosophical Grammar*, Noah Webster pays homage to national usage by accepting *you was* because "national usage determines correctness in grammar."

4. I know", she said, "that you are telling me a barefaced lie."

rewrite:

"I know," she said, "that you are telling me a barefaced lie."

The placement of the period and the comma in relation to the closing quotation mark is a clear case where usage, rather than logic, has established the prevailing convention. Many reputable British editors and publishers put the period or comma *outside* the closing quotation mark, especially when the quotation marks enclose something less than a complete sentence—e.g., a word or a phrase, as in sentences 1 and 2. But the American convention is almost universally to put the period or comma *inside* the closing quotation mark.

The advantage of such consistency is that you never have to pause and ask yourself, "Is this a case where the period goes inside or outside the quotation mark?" Whether it is a single word or a phrase or a dependent clause or an independent clause, the period or comma *always* goes inside the closing quotation mark.

In handwriting or in typewriting, take care to put the period or comma clearly *inside* the quotation mark, not *under* it, as in two instances in sentence 4. In the case of a quotation within a quotation, both the single-stroke quotation mark and the double-stroke quotation mark go *outside* the period or the comma, as in this example:

"I read recently," he said, "that Patrick Henry never said, 'Give me liberty or give me death.'"

80

81 Quotation Marks with Colon and Semicolon

The colon or semicolon always goes outside the closing quotation mark.

”: ”;

Examples of a misplaced colon or semicolon in relation to the closing quotation mark:

1. The participants in the seminar considered the following sequence of activities a "normal load:" working, eating, exercising, studying, and sleeping.

rewrite:

   The participants in the seminar considered the following sequence of activities a "normal load": working, eating, exercising, studying, and sleeping.

2. Mr. Moulton told the workers, "Continue to walk the picket line;" yet even as he gave that advice, he was fearful of what the strikebreakers would do.

rewrite:

   Mr. Moulton told the workers, "Continue to walk the picket line"; yet even as he gave that advice, he was fearful of what the strikebreakers would do.

Whereas the period or the comma always goes *inside* the closing quotation mark, the colon or the semicolon always goes *outside* it. Whenever writers have occasion to use quotation marks with a colon or a semicolon, they have only to recall that the convention governing the placement of the colon or the semicolon in relation to the closing quotation mark is just the opposite of the convention for the placement of the period and the comma.

81

82 Quotation Marks with the Question Mark

The question mark sometimes goes inside, sometimes outside, the closing quotation mark.

?"   "?

Examples of the question mark placed wrongly in relation to the closing quotation mark:

1. The students asked the physicist, "What makes it spin"?

rewrite:
   The students asked the physicist, "What makes it spin?"

2. What official said, "You will not manipulate your statistics to make them say what you want them to say?"

rewrite:
   What official said, "You will not manipulate your statistics to make them say what you want them to say"?

3. When will they stop asking, "Who is responsible for falsifying these vital statistics"?

rewrite:
   When will they stop asking, "Who is responsible for falsifying these vital statistics?"

82

Although a period or a comma always goes inside the closing quotation mark and a colon or a semicolon always goes outside the closing quotation mark, you have to consider the individual case before deciding whether to put the question mark inside or outside the closing quotation mark. Fortunately, the criteria for determining whether the question mark goes inside or outside the quotation mark are fairly simple to apply:

(a) When the whole sentence but not the unit enclosed in quotation marks is a question, the quotation mark goes *outside* the closing quotation mark. (See sentence **2**.)

(b) When only the unit enclosed in quotation marks is a question, the question mark goes *inside* the closing quotation mark. (See sentence 1.)

(c) When the whole sentence and the unit enclosed in quotation marks are both questions, the question mark goes *inside* the closing quotation mark. (See sentence 3.)

Whenever the question mark occurs at the end of a sentence, it serves as the terminal punctuation for the entire sentence. In (b), for instance, you do not add a period outside the closing quotation mark, and in (c), you do not need to add another question mark outside the closing quotation mark.

83 Titles, Underlined

The titles of books, newspapers, magazines, professional journals, plays, long poems, movies, radio programs, television programs, long musical compositions, works of art, and the names of ships and airplanes should be <u>underlined</u>.

83

Examples of titles that should be underlined:

1. Before you write your paper, you should read Thomas Pearsall and Donald Cunningham's book "How to Write for the World of Work."

rewrite:

   Before you write your paper, you should read Thomas Pearsall and Donald Cunningham's book <u>How to Write for the World of Work</u>.
   (*underline the title of a book*)

2. I learned of your opening for an electrical engineer through your advertisement in the Cleveland Plain Dealer.

rewrite:

> I learned of your opening for an electrical engineer through your advertisement in the <u>Cleveland Plain Dealer</u>.
> (*underline the title of a newspaper, a magazine, or a journal*)

3. The class learned a great deal about technical writing from watching "60 Minutes" on television last Sunday.

rewrite:

> The class learned a great deal about technical writing from watching <u>60 Minutes</u> on television last Sunday.
> (*underline the title of a television show*)

4. Charles Darwin took a historic trip on the Beagle.

rewrite:

> Charles Darwin took a historic trip on the <u>Beagle</u>.
> (*underline the name of a ship*)

Printers use *italics*—a special typeface that slants slightly to the right—to set off certain words in a sentence (or certain sentences in a paragraph) from the body of words or sentences that are printed in roman type (upright letters). The word *italics* in this and the previous sentence is printed in italics. When you write by hand or on a typewriter or on a word processor, you signify italicized words by <u>underlining</u> them.

One of the uses of italic type is to set off the words that appear in certain kinds of names and titles. Most often, you have occasion to use italics for the titles of book-length or pamphlet-length published materials. Besides being a convention, the use of italics for titles can also protect meaning in some instances. If, for instance, you wrote "I don't really like Huckleberry Finn," a reader might be uncertain (unless the context gave a clue) whether you were revealing a dislike for Mark Twain's novel or for the character of that name in that novel. Simply by underlining (italicizing) the proper name, you could indicate unambiguously that you disliked the novel, not the character.

How do you decide whether a poem is long enough to

have its title underlined? As with most relative matters, the extreme cases are easily determinable. Obviously, a sonnet (a fourteen-line poem) would not qualify as a long poem, but Milton's *Paradise Lost* would. It is the middle-length poem that causes indecision. A reliable rule of thumb is this: if the poem was ever published as a separate book or if it could conceivably be published as a separate book, it can be considered long enough to have its title underlined. But if you cannot decide whether a poem is "long" or "short," either underline the title or enclose it in quotation marks and use that system consistently through the paper.

84 Titles in Quotation Marks

The titles of articles, essays, short poems, songs, chapters of books, short stories, and episodes of radio and television programs should be enclosed in quotation marks.

84

Examples of titles that need to be enclosed with quotation marks:

1. Thomas Gray's Elegy Written in a Country Churchyard is reputed to be the most anthologized poem in the English language.

rewrite:

Thomas Gray's "Elegy Written in a Country Churchyard" is reputed to be the most anthologized poem in the English language.

(*quotation marks for the title of a short poem*)

2. Carol Lipson's Technical Communication: The Cultural Context appeared in the Fall 1986 issue of the Technical Writing Teacher.

rewrite:

Carol Lipson's "Technical Communication: The Cultural Context" appeared in the Fall 1986 issue of the Technical Writing Teacher.

(quotation marks for the title of an article in a journal)

3. Amazing Grace may be the favorite religious hymn in Protestant churches in the United States.

rewrite:

"Amazing Grace" may be the favorite religious hymn in Protestant churches in the United States.

(quotation marks for the title of a song)

4. I never heard my father laugh as hard as he did the night he heard the sketch Tomato Butt on Garrison Keillor's A Prairie Home Companion.

rewrite:

I never heard my father laugh as hard as he did the night he heard the sketch "Tomato Butt" on Garrison Keillor's A Prairie Home Companion.

(quotation marks for the title of an episode on a radio or a TV program)

84 The general rule here is that the titles of material that is *part* of a book or a periodical or a program should be enclosed in quotation marks.

For the title of a paper or a report or a proposal that you write, follow the instructions you are given about the format of the title. But if you are not given explicit instructions about the format of the title, do not underline or enclose the title of your paper in quotation marks. If your title contains elements that are normally underlined or enclosed in quotation marks, those elements, of course, should be underlined or enclosed in quotation marks.

The conventional formats of a title of a paper submitted as a class assignment or for publication are illustrated here in typescript:

WRONG:

"The Significance of Linguistics for Technical Writing"

The Significance of Linguistics for Technical Writing

THE SIGNIFICANCE OF LINGUISTICS FOR TECHNICAL WRITING

RIGHT:

The Significance of Linguistics for Technical Writing

The Meaning of the Terms <u>Hardware</u> and <u>Software</u> in Computer Language

An Assessment of an Important New Book, <u>Writing in the Arts and Sciences</u>

"One Giant Step for Mankind"—Historic Words for a Historic Occasion

85 Italicize Words as Words

<u>Underline</u> (*italicize*) words referred to as words.

Examples of words that should be <u>underlined</u> (*italicized*):

1. The class challenged my account of the origin of integrity.

rewrite:

> The class challenged my account of the origin of <u>integrity</u>.

2. Many of the people who participated in my survey said later that they did not know what inferred meant, although the statistics do not support that revelation.

rewrite:

> Many of the people who participated in my survey said later that they did not know what <u>inferred</u> meant, although the statistics do not support that revelation.

3. The term metaphysical poets was invented by John Dryden and was adopted by Dr. Samuel Johnson to designate a certain class of seventeenth-century poets.

rewrite:

> The term <u>metaphysical poets</u> was invented by John Dryden and was adopted by Dr. Samuel Johnson to designate a certain class of seventeenth-century poets.

4. The dictionary defines "delirium" as a more or less temporary disorder of the mental faculties.

rewrite:

> The dictionary defines <u>delirium</u> as "a more or less temporary disorder of the mental faculties."

85   One of the uses of the graphic device of underlining (italics) is to distinguish a word being used as a *word* from that same word used as a symbol for a thing or an idea. Looking at sentence **1**, we can see the difference in meaning created by underlining or not underlining some word in a sentence:

> The class challenged my account of the origin of integrity.

> The class challenged my account of the origin of <u>integrity</u>.

Both of these sentences have the same words in the same order. The only difference between them is that in the second sentence, one of the words is underlined (italicized). That underlining of the word **integrity** makes for a difference in the meaning of the two sentences. The first sentence signifies that what is being challenged is the account of the origin of the *thing* (the abstract quality) designated by the word **integrity**; the second sentence signifies that what is being questioned is the account of the origin of the *word* **integrity**. Underlining (italicizing) the word **integrity** helps the reader read the sentence as the writer intended it to be read—namely, that it was the word, not the virtue, that was being questioned.

An alternative but less common device for marking words used as words is to enclose the words in quotation marks, as was done in sentence **4** above:

> The dictionary defines the word "delirium" as a more or less temporary disorder of the mental faculties.

Since both devices, underlining and quotation marks, are authorized by convention, you should adopt one system and use it consistently. The use of underlining (italics) is probably the safer of the two systems, however, because quotation marks are also used to enclose quoted definitions of a word, as in the revision of sentence **4**, and to enclose quoted words or phrases, as in the sentence

> We heard her say "yes."

Here, **yes** is not being referred to as a word but is a quotation of what she said.

86 Italicize Foreign Words

Underline (*italicize*) foreign words and phrases, unless they have become naturalized or Anglicized.

Examples of foreign words and phrases that should be <u>underlined</u> (*italicized*):

1. It was reasonable for the customer to ask whether our collateral was an adequate "quid pro quo" for the concession that he had made in signing the contract.

rewrite:

It was reasonable for the customer to ask whether our collateral was an adequate <u>quid pro quo</u> for the concession that he had made in signing the contract.

2. Our French subsidiary considered our questioning of its fiscal responsibility to be an instance of lèse-majesté.

rewrite:

Our French subsidiary considered our questioning of its fiscal responsibility to be an instance of <u>lèse-majesté.</u>

3. The handsome gaucho always greeted us with a cheery "buenos días."

rewrite:

The handsome gaucho always greeted us with a cheery <u>buenos días.</u>

4. There has been a pronounced revival in Germany of the Weltschmerz that once characterized the mood of the nineteenth-century Romantic poets.

rewrite:

There has been a pronounced revival in Germany of the <u>Weltschmerz</u> that once characterized the mood of the nineteenth-century Romantic poets.

So that the reader will not be even momentarily mystified by the sudden intrusion of strange-looking words into a stream of English words, writers use underlining (italics) to indicate foreign words and phrases. The graphic device of underlining or italics does not ensure, of course, that the reader will be able to translate the foreign expression, but it does prevent confusion by alerting the reader to the presence of non-English words.

86

Some foreign words and phrases, such as habeas corpus, divorcée, mania, siesta, and subpoena, have been used so often in an English context that they have been accepted into the vocabulary as "naturalized" or "Anglicized" words and therefore do not need to be underlined (italicized). Since dictionaries have a system of indicating which foreign words and phrases have become naturalized and which have not, you should consult a dictionary when you are in doubt about the current status of a particular foreign word or phrase.

An exception to the rule is that proper nouns designating foreign persons, places, institutions, even when they retain their native spelling and pronunciation, are *always* set forth without underlining (*italics*). For example, none of the French proper nouns in the following sentence should be underlined (*italicized*): "Pierre Chardin thought that the Bibliothèque Nationale was on the Champs Élysées in Paris."

87 Hyphen for Compound Words

Compound words should be hyphenated.

Examples of compound words that need to be hyphenated:

1. While you are running around campus trying to complete your registration, you are missing out on all the important first day information being dispensed in the classroom.

rewrite:

While you are running around campus trying to complete

your registration, you are missing out on all the important first-day information being dispensed in the classroom.

2. After forty five minutes, one of the secretaries came back with his transcript.

rewrite:

After forty-five minutes, one of the secretaries came back with his transcript.

3. They scheduled the examination in three quarter hour segments.

rewrite:

They scheduled the examination in three quarter-hour segments.

4. The coil bending operation in that department is, in its present form, highly inefficient.

rewrite:

The coil-bending operation in that department is, in its present form, highly inefficient.

5. A five or six story building should be all you need for that kind of plant operation.

rewrite:

A five- or six-story building should be all you need for that kind of plant operation.

6. They were much impressed by her never say die attitude.

rewrite:

They were much impressed by her never-say-die attitude.

7. Jim Paisley was the only new car dealer in town.

rewrite:

Jim Paisley was the only new-car dealer in town.

English reveals its Germanic origin in its tendency to form compounds—that is, to take two or more words and join them to create a single unit that designates a thing or a concept quite different from what the individual words designate. A familiar example is the word *basketball*. When the two distinct words *basket* and *ball* were first joined to designate an athletic game or the kind of ball used in that game, the words were linked by a hyphen: basket-ball. When repeated use had made this new compound familiar to readers, the hyphen was dropped, and the two words were printed as a single word, with no break between the two constituent parts.

Dozens of words in English have made this transition from a hyphenated compound to a single amalgamated word (e.g., airport, skyscraper, briefcase). But hundreds of compounds are still printed with a hyphen, either because they have not been used enough to achieve status as unmarked hybrids or because the absence of a hyphen would lead to ambiguity. A reliable dictionary will indicate which compounds have made the passage and which have not.

With the exception of those words that have become recognized amalgams, a hyphen should be used to link the following:

(a) two or more words functioning as a single grammatical unit.

> his **better-late-than-never** disposition (adjective)
> the junkyard had a huge **car-crusher** (noun)
> the hoodlum **pistol-whipped** him (verb)
> he conceded the point **willy-nilly** (adverb)

87

(b) two-word numbers (from 21 to 99) when they are written out.

> **twenty-one**, **thirty-six**, **forty-eight**, **ninety-nine**

(c) combinations with prefixes ex- and self-

> **ex-president**, **ex-wife**, **self-denial**, **self-contradictory**

(d) combinations with prefixes like **anti-**, **pro-**, **pre-**, **post-**, when the second element in the combinations begins with a capital letter or a number.

> **anti-Establishment**, **pro-American**, **pre-1929**, **post-1985**

(e) combinations with prefixes like **anti-**, **pro-**, **pre-**, **re-**, **semi-**, **sub-**, **over-**, when the second element begins with the same letter that occurs at the end of the prefix.

> **anti-intellectual**, **pro-oxidant**, **pre-election**, **re-entry**, **over-refined**, **semi-independent**, **sub-basement**

(f) combinations where the unhyphenated compound might be mistaken for another word.

> **re-cover** (the chair)
> **recover** (the lost wallet)
> **re-sign** (the contract)
> **resign** (the office)
> **co-op** (a co-operative apartment)
> **coop** (a pen for chickens)

With the exceptions noted in **(d)** and **(e)**, compounds formed with prefixes now tend to be written as a single word (for example, **antiknock**, **nonrestrictive**, **preconscious**, **subdivision**, **postgraduate**). From extensive reading, one develops a sense for the compounds that have been used often enough to become a single word in English.

Frequently in writing, only a hyphen will clarify ambiguous syntax. In sentence **3**, for instance, a reader would have difficulty determining whether the examination was divided into three segments of fifteen minutes each (a meaning that would be clearly signaled by this placement of the hyphen: **three quarter-hour segments**) or whether it was divided into segments of 45-minute duration (a meaning that is clearly signaled by this placement of the hyphen: **three-quarter-hour segments**). There is a similar ambiguity in sentence **7**. Only a hyphen will clarify whether Jim Paisley is a **new-car dealer** or a **new car-dealer**.

Sentence **5** shows how to hyphenate a compound when there is more than one term on the left side of the hyphenation (**five-, six-**). In this way, **story** need not be repeated (as in **a five-story or a six-story building**). In typing, insert a space after the hyphen if the hyphen is not immediately followed by the word it is meant to join (**five- or six-story**, *not* **five-or six-story**).

88 Hyphen to Divide Words

A word can be broken and hyphenated at the end of a line only at a syllable-break; a one-syllable word can never be broken and hyphenated.

Examples of words improperly syllabified:

1. bell-igerent	*rewrite:*	bel-ligerent
2. part-icular	*rewrite:*	par-ticular
3. stopp-ing	*rewrite:*	stop-ping
4. Eng-lish	*rewrite:*	En-glish
5. wrench-cd	*rewrite:*	wrenched
6. a-bout	*rewrite:*	about
7. diffe-rent	*rewrite:*	differ-ent
8. sanct-imony	*rewrite:*	sanc-timony

88

For the writer, two valuable bits of information are supplied by the initial entry of every word in the dictionary: (1) the spelling of the word, (2) the syllabification of the word. Words of more than two syllables can be broken and hyphenated at more than one place. The word **belligerent**, for instance, is entered this way in the dictionary: **bel·lig·er·ent**. If that word occurred at the end of a line and you saw that you could not get the whole word in the remaining space, you could break the word and hyphenate it at any of the syllables marked with a raised period. But you may not break the word in any of the following places: **bell·igerent, belli·gerent, bellige·rent**.

Since the syllabification of English words is often unpredictable, it is safest to consult a dictionary when you are in doubt about where the syllable-breaks occur. But after a while, you learn certain "tricks" about syllabification that save you a trip to the dictionary. A word can usually be broken as follows:

(a) after a prefix (**con-, ad-, un-, im-**)

(b) before a suffix (**-tion, -ment, -less, -ous, -ing**)

(c) between double consonants (**oc-cur-rence, cop-per, stop-ping, prig-gish**)

One-syllable words, however, can never be divided and hyphenated, no matter how long they are. So if you come to the end of a line and find that you do not have enough space to squeeze in single-syllable words like **horde**, **grieve**, **stopped**, **quaint**, **strength**, **wrenched**, leave the space blank and write the whole word on the next line. You have no choice in this case.

Even in the interest of preserving a right-hand margin, you should not divide a word so that only one or two letters of it stand at the end of the line or at the beginning of the next line. Faced with divisions like **a-bout**, **o-cean**, **un-healthy**, **grass-y**, **dioram-a**, **flor-id**, **smok-er**, **live-ly**, you should put the whole word on that line or on the next line. Remember that the hyphen itself takes up one space.

89

89 Numbers

Observe the conventions governing the use of numbers in written copy.

Examples of violations of the conventions:

1. 612 applicants showed up on the first day.

rewrite:
> **Six hundred and twelve** applicants showed up on the first day.
> **or**
> A total of **612** applicants showed up on the first day.

2. Every one of these 42 verbs appears from time to time in the revered literary writing of that era.

rewrite:
> Every one of these **forty-two** verbs appears from time to time in the revered literary writing of that era.

3. When I was only 5 years old, I could ride a horse.

rewrite:
> When I was only **five** years old, I could ride a horse.

4. The shelf was six feet four inches long.

rewrite:
> The shelf was **6 ft. 4 in.** long.

5. The auction started at four P.M. in the afternoon.

rewrite:
> The auction started at **4:00** P.M.
> **or**
> The auction started at **four o'clock in the afternoon.**

6. About six % of the stores were selling a gross of three-by-five index cards for more than thirty-six dollars and thirty cents.

rewrite:
> About **6%** of the stores were selling a gross of **3" × 5"** cards for more than **$36.30.**

The most common conventions governing the use of numbers in written copy are as follows:

(a) Do not begin a sentence with an Arabic numeral; spell out the number or recast the sentence (see sentence **1**).

(b) Spell out any number of less than three digits (or any

89

number under 101) when the number is used as an adjective modifying a noun (see sentences **2** and **3**).

(c) Always use Arabic numerals with **a.m.** and **p.m.** (or **A.M.** and **P.M.**) and do not add the redundant **o'clock** and **morning** or **afternoon** (see sentence **5**).

(d) Use Arabic numerals for dates and page numbers.

(e) Use Arabic numerals for addresses (618 N. 29th St.), dollars and cents ($4.68, $0.15 or 15 cents), decimals (3.14, 0.475), degrees (52°F, 26°C), measurements (especially when abbreviations are used: 3" × 5", 3.75 mi., 2 ft. 9 in., 6'2" tall, but **six feet tall**), percentages (6% or 6 percent, but always use **percent** with fractional percentages: 6½ percent or 6.5 percent) (see sentence **6**).

90 Capitalization

Observe the conventions governing the capitalization of certain words.

Examples of words that need to be capitalized:

1. On Tuesday, president George Bush informed the members of congress that he was nominating judge David Souter for the vacancy in the supreme court of the United States.

   rewrite:

   On Tuesday, **P**resident George Bush informed the members of **C**ongress that he was nominating **J**udge David Souter for the vacancy in the **S**upreme **C**ourt of the United States.

2. The title of the article in *Scientific American* was "Recent developments in rocket-propulsion fuels."

   The title of the article in *Scientific American* was "**R**ecent **D**evelopments in **R**ocket-**P**ropulsion **F**uels."

3. Dr. Truong Lehang, a renowned professor in the department of marine biology at this Canadian university, has been studying the migratory habits of whales in the arctic, the northeast, and the pacific northwest.

rewrite:

Dr. Truong Lehang, a renowned professor in the Department of Marine Biology at this Canadian university, has been studying the migratory habits of whales in the Arctic, the Northeast, and the Pacific Northwest.

4. The prime vacation time for most Americans is the period between the fourth of July and labor day.

rewrite:

The prime vacation time for most Americans is the period between the Fourth of July and Labor Day.

In general, the convention governing capitalization is that the first letter of the proper name (that is, the particular or exclusive name) of persons, places, things, institutions, agencies, nations, and such should be capitalized. While the tendency today is to use lowercase letters for many words that formerly were written or printed with capital letters (for instance, *biblical reference* instead of ***Biblical reference***), the use of capital letters still prevails in the written medium in the following cases:

90

(a) The first letter of the first word of a sentence.

They were uncertain about which words should be capitalized.

(b) The first letter of the first word of every line of traditional English verse.

Little fly,
Thy summer's play
My thoughtless hand
Has brushed away.

(c) All nouns, pronouns, verbs, adjectives, adverbs, and

the first and last words of titles of publications and other artistic works.

> *Remembrance of Things Past* (see **83**)
> "The Place of the Enthymeme in Rhetorical Theory" (see **84**)
> "A Tent That Families Can Live In"
> *The Return of the Pink Panther*

(d) The first name, middle name or initial, and last name of a person, real or fictional.

T. S. Eliot	**Sylvia Marie Mikkelsen**
David Copperfield	**Achilles**

(e) The names and abbreviations of villages, towns, cities, counties, states, nations, and regions.

Chillicothe, Ohio	**Cook County**
U.S.A.	**Soviet Union**
Indochina	**Arctic Circle**
the **Western** world	**South America**
the **Midwestern** states	the **South** (but: we drove south)

(f) The names of rivers, lakes, falls, oceans, mountains, deserts, parks.

the **Mississippi River**	**Atlantic**
the **Grand Tetons**	**Yellowstone National Park**
Lake Erie	**Victoria Falls**

(g) The names and abbreviations of businesses, industries, institutions, agencies, schools, political parties, religious denominations, and philosophical, scientific, literary, and artistic movements.

Creighton University	**Democrats**
the **Republican** convention	**C.I.A.**
Dow Chemical Corporation	**HarperCollins Publishers**

90

Communist (but: a communist ideology)

Victorian literature

Thomistic philosophy

Methodist

Smithsonian Institution

the Nuclear Age

Japan Air Lines

the Pentagon

Buddhism

(h) The titles of historical events, epochs, and periods.

Renaissance

World War II

the Middle Ages

Reformation

Thirty Years' War

Ice Age

the Battle of Gettysburg

the Depression

(i) Honorary and official titles when they precede the name of a person.

Rabbi Balfour Brickner

the Duke of Cornwall

Pope John Paul II

His (Her) Excellency

Bishop Tsuji

General Patton

Chief Justice Brennan

Queen Elizabeth

(j) The names of weekdays, months, holidays, holy days, and other special days or periods.

Christmas Eve

Passover

Lent

Mardi Gras

Memorial Day

the Fourth of July

National Book Week

the first Sunday in June

(k) The names and abbreviations of the books and divisions of the Bible and other sacred books (no italics for these titles).

Genesis

Lk. (Gospel of Luke)

Epistles to the Romans

King James Version

Talmud

Pentateuch

Acts of the Apostles

Koran

Scriptures

Bhagavad Gita

90

Book of **J**ob   **L**otus **S**utra
Pss. (**P**salms)   **S**cience and **H**ealth

Exceptions: Do *not* capitalize words like the underlined in
the following examples:

the African <u>coast</u> (but: the   the <u>river</u> Elbe (but: the Elbe
West Coast)   River)

<u>northern</u> Wisconsin   the <u>federal</u> <u>government</u>

the <u>senator</u> from Wyoming   the <u>presidential</u> itinerary

the <u>municipal</u> <u>library</u>   the <u>county</u> <u>courthouse</u>

in the <u>autumn</u>   they headed <u>west</u>

90

FORMAT OF THE RESEARCH PAPER

GENERAL INSTRUCTIONS

A research paper reports the results of some investigation, experiment, interview, or reading that you have done. Some of the ordinary papers you write are also based on personal investigations, interviews, and reading, and when your paper is based on data derived from research, you should acknowledge the source of the data. For instance, you can reveal the source of information or quotations by saying, right in the text of your paper, "Mr. Stanley Smith, the director of the Upward Bound project, with whom I talked last week, confirmed the rumor that. . . ." or "James Reston said in his column in last Sunday's *New York Times* that. . . ." Authors of research papers also use identifying lead-ins like those, but in addition, they supply—usually in parenthetical references—any further information (such as the exact date of the newspaper they are quoting from and the number of the page from which the quotation was taken) that readers would need if they wanted to check the sources. By revealing this specific information about the source, authors enable readers to check the accuracy and fairness of the reporting, and they enhance their credibility with readers.

157

In the pages that follow, we will present some advice about gathering and reporting material from outside sources, some models of parenthetical forms, and a sample research paper. The instructor or the publication that you write for may prescribe a format that differs from the advice given here, but if no specific instructions are given, you can follow these suggestions and models with the assurance that they conform to the prevailing conventions for research papers written in most fields. The format for documenting references, citations, and quotations may differ slightly from discipline to discipline, but whether you are writing a research paper in the humanities or in the physical sciences, the same kind of basic information about the sources is supplied in the documentation.

A   Selecting an Appropriate Subject

Taking special care in selecting an appropriate subject for your research paper will, in the long run, make the task of writing the paper easier and increase your chances of getting a good grade for your efforts. Sometimes you will have a completely free choice of a subject for your paper; at other times your instructor will set up a list of subjects or a general category of subjects from which you must choose. In either case, the ultimate choice of a specific subject will be yours. Make this choice conscientiously and judiciously.

A number of considerations will guide you in selecting an appropriate subject: (1) the physical limits set for the paper, either in terms of the number of words (e.g., 2500–3000 words) or in terms of the number of pages (e.g., 8–10 pages); (2) the time available to you, from the initial assignment to the final due date; (3) your particular interests; (4) the research facilities available to you; (5) the defined limits of the subject; and (6) a determination of the main point you want to make about the subject you choose.

Suppose that from a list of topics suggested by your instructor, you chose this one: The Use of Computers in the Schools. You chose that subject partly because it interests you (3) and partly because you are sure that your school library contains lots of material on this timely subject (4). Because you have only five weeks in which to do the research and write the paper (2) and because the instructor set a limit of 2000–2500 words (8–10 double-spaced pages at 250 words per page) for the paper (1), you realize that you must narrow the broad subject that you have chosen (5) and determine the main point you want to make about the narrowed subject that you finally select (6).

By chipping away at your broad subject, you can get it down to manageable proportions. You decide that you do not want to consider all the possible uses of computers in the schools, so you confine yourself to word processors. *Schools* is too broad a category for this paper, so you decide to concentrate on the undergraduate college scene. You further narrow the subject by specifying the use of the word processor in the college freshman composition classroom. Now that you have a sharply defined subject (5) that can be managed within the limits set for you (1, 2, 3, 4), you must decide what point you want to make about that subject (6). After careful deliberation, you settle on a focus and decide to formulate that focus in a statement of purpose rather than in a thesis sentence: I want to investigate some of the successes that colleges in the United States have had in improving the writing of students by using word processors in freshman composition courses.

A

Now you are ready to go to the library to find some usable material on that sharply defined topic.

B   Using the Library

Unless your research paper is simply a report of a lab experiment, a questionnaire, or a series of interviews that you conducted, it will depend largely on your reading of books and articles. The main source of books and articles is the library—either the public library or the college library. Perhaps the chief benefit that you derive from doing a research paper is that this exercise forces you to become acquainted with the library and its resources. Becoming aware of the wealth of knowledge stored in the library and getting to know *where* the various pockets of wealth are located in the library and *how* to use them will be a valuable part of your general education.

The best way to get acquainted with the library is to visit it, to look around, to examine the card catalogue, to take some books down off the shelves and open them, and, above all, to *use the library*. But if you want to speed up the getting-acquainted process, you can consult a book like Eugene P. Sheehy's *A Guide to Reference Books*, which you can find on the reference shelves of the library. (The 10th edition was published in 1986 by the American Library Association of Chicago.) What follows is an introduction to a few general reference sources and some bibliographical sources, which would be both generally helpful in your pursuit of knowledge and particularly helpful to you in preparing to write a research paper.

GENERAL REFERENCE SOURCES

Encyclopedias

Multivolume encyclopedias are the most familiar and usually the most available source of information on a wide range of subjects. The treatment of topics in an encyclopedia varies in length from a few sentences to several pages, though many of the entries, especially the longer ones, list pertinent books and articles that you can consult for further information.

The encyclopedia is a good starting point for a research project, but ordinarily it should not be the stopping point. You will have to go on to more specialized reference sources. Here are three well-known multivolume encyclopedias and one very useful single-volume encyclopedia. All of them cover a wide range of subjects, are international in their scope, and cover all centuries, but each one is strong in a particular area. The first two publish yearbooks, which cover the main events and topics of the previous year.

Encyclopedia Americana. Danbury, CT: Grolier Educational Corp., 1985. 30 volumes. Particularly useful for anything connected with the United States.

Encyclopaedia Britannica. Chicago: Encyclopaedia Britannica Educational Corp., 1984. 30 volumes. Strong on both American and British topics.

Chambers's Encyclopedia. Elmsford, NY: Maxwell Scientific International, 1973. 15 volumes. Particularly strong on British topics.

The New Columbia Encyclopedia. 4th ed. New York: Columbia University Press, 1975. One volume. More than 50,000 articles on the humanities, social sciences, life and physical sciences, and geography packed into 3,052 pages.

B

Almanacs and Other General Sources of Facts and Statistics

Almanacs are a rich storehouse of factual and statistical information. They always retain the basic historical, geographical, social, political, and statistical information, but each year they add the pertinent factual and statistical information for the previous year. Here are the titles of two inexpensive paperback almanacs and the titles of two other sources of facts and statistics that can be found in the reference room of the library:

Information Please Almanac. New York: Simon and Schuster, 1947–
Published annually.

World Almanac. New York: Newspaper Enterprise Association, Inc.,
1868–   . Published annually.

Facts on File. New York: Facts on File, Inc., 1940–   . Published weekly.
A valuable source of information about the important events of the
week.

U.S. Bureau of the Census: Statistical Abstract of the United States. Washington,
D.C.: Government Printing Office, 1879–   . Published annually.
The most comprehensive source of statistical information about all
aspects of American life.

Handbooks

Another source of general information about a particular field is the one-volume reference work that we will label *handbook*. Handbooks contain some of the same kinds of information supplied by multivolume encyclopedias, but the entries are shorter, and they are restricted to a special field, like literature or business. But precisely because they are restricted to a particular field, they often cover topics that are considered too minor or specialized for inclusion in a multivolume encyclopedia. In a handbook, you can expect to find these kinds of information about the field covered: definitions of key terms and concepts; identifications of allusions; accounts of historical or ideological movements; short biographical sketches; summaries of important books; bibliographies. Here is a list of a few important handbooks, one for each of seven different fields.

The Reader's Encyclopedia. Ed. William R. Benet. 3rd ed. New York: Crowell, 1987. A handbook of world literature.

Oxford Companion to the Theatre. Ed. Phyllis Hartnoll. 4th ed. New York: Oxford University Press, 1985. A handy reference source for information about world drama, from its beginnings in ancient Greece.

Oxford Companion to Film. Ed. Liz-Anne Bawden. New York: Oxford University Press, 1976. One of the many "Oxford Companions," about an art form that has become a prominent part of everyday life.

Encyclopedia of Banking and Finance. Ed. Ferdinand L. Garcia 8th ed. Boston: The Bankers Publishing Co., 1983. An invaluable one-volume reference work for anything connected with business.

The Concise Encyclopedia of Western Philosophy and Philosophers. Ed. J. O. Urmson. New York: Hawthorn Books, 1989. Brief but authoritative information about philosophy and philosophers.

Dictionary of Education. Ed. Carter V. Good. 3rd ed. New York: McGraw-Hill, 1973. More than a dictionary, this reference work supplies the usual kind of handbook information about the field of professional education.

International Cyclopedia of Music and Musicians. Ed. Bruce Bohle. 10th ed. New York: Dodd, Mead, 1975. One of a number of very good one-volume handbooks on music.

Biographical Dictionaries

Encyclopedias and handbooks will provide you with brief biographical sketches of prominent men and women. But for fuller accounts of persons, both living and deceased, and for biographical sketches of less prominent people, you will have to go to the more specialized biographical dictionaries. Listed below are five of the best-known and most useful of these specialized biographical dictionaries.

Dictionary of National Biography (sometimes referred to as the *DNB*). New York: Oxford University Press, 1921. 22 volumes (a reissue of the original 66-volume set published in 1885). Lives of about 18,000 *deceased* subjects of Great Britain and Commonwealth dependencies. Supplements bring the coverage up to 1970.

Who's Who. London: A & C Black, Ltd., 1849–   . Published annually. Biographical information about distinguished *living* men and women of Great Britain.

Dictionary of American Biography (sometimes referred to as the *DAB*). New York: Scribner's. 1927–1981. 17 volumes. The equivalent of the British *DNB*, this multivolume set gives the biographies of prominent and not-so-prominent *deceased* Americans.

Who's Who in America. Chicago: Marquis, 1899–   Published every second year. The equivalent of the British *Who's Who*, this reference source provides biographical information about notable *living* Americans.

International Who's Who. London: Europa Publications, 1935–   . Published annually. Information about the lives of prominent *living* men and women of all nations.

SPECIALIZED BIBLIOGRAPHIES

The reference works mentioned in the previous sections can give you general information that could be useful for your personal enlightenment or for your classwork. But since a research paper is usually written about a narrow topic in a specialized field, you will need more specific information than those general reference works can provide. You must track down books, articles, pamphlets, and monographs that deal more particularly with the topic of your paper. To track down that more specific material, you can turn to *bibliographical reference works*—works that list the authors or editors, titles, and publication information of published books, articles, and reviews on a particular topic. Fortunately, there are a number of general and specialized bibliographical guides.

A helpful guide to available bibliographies is the *Bibliographic Index* (New York: H. W. Wilson, 1937–   ). This guide to the bibliographies that have been published in books, pamphlets, bulletins, and periodicals is arranged alphabetically according to subject. If you were doing a research paper on the trucking industry, for example, and wanted to find out whether any bibliographies on this subject had been published, you could consult several volumes of the *Bibliographic Index* under the main subject-heading of *Transportation.* If you found a bibliography listed there on the trucking industry, you would then have to check the card catalogue to find out whether your library had that bibliography. Once you got your hands on that bibliography, you would find an extensive list of books and articles dealing with the trucking industry. Then you would once again have to consult the card catalogue to see whether your library had any of the books and articles listed in that bibliography.

PERIODICAL INDEXES

Of more practical use, perhaps, to the undergraduate or informal researcher are the general and specialized indexes to reviews and articles in popular magazines and newspapers and in various scholarly journals.

General Periodical Indexes

Book Review Digest. 1905–   . Summarizes reviews of books from a large number of periodicals. Gives critical reception of books reviewed.

Nineteenth Century Reader's Guide. 1890–1899. Periodicals for the iast ten years of the 1800s.

Readers' Guide to Periodical Literature. 1900–   . An excellent guide for general purpose reading. Lists articles from a broad range of periodicals. Entries are by author, subject, and cross-listing. Most articles written for general public.

Specialized Periodical Indexes

Art Index. 1929–

Biological and Agricultural Index. 1964–   . Supersedes *Agricultural Index,* 1916–1964.

Business Periodicals Index. 1958–   . Supersedes *Industrial Arts Index,* 1913–1957.

Education Index. 1929–   .

General Science Index. 1978–   .

Humanities Index. 1974–   . Formerly *International Index,* 1907–1965, and *Social Sciences and Humanities Index,* 1965–1974.

Music Index. 1949–   .

Public Affairs Information Service Bulletin. 1915–   .

Social Sciences Index. 1974–   . Formerly *International Index,* 1907–1965 and *Social Sciences and Humanities Index,* 1965–1974.

United States Government Publications, Monthly Catalog. 1895–   .

MICROFORMS AND DATABASES

Besides the printed indexes to periodical literature, there are indexes recorded in such miniaturized forms as microfilms and microfiches and in on-line computerized databases. Whereas the printed indexes lag behind the current date anywhere from three months to a whole year, the indexes recorded in some of the electronic media can be frequently and easily updated so that they lag behind the current date by as little as a month. So if you need to compile a list of articles on a current topic, the indexes in microforms and databases may be your only resource.

The two microfilm indexes to periodical literature that you are most likely to find in your college or public library are the *Magazine Index* (Belmont, CA: Information Access Corporation) and the *National Newspaper Index* (Belmont, CA: Information Access Corporation). *Magazine Index,* which covers the most recent four years, indexes more than 400 magazines published in North America. In this alphabetical index, items are listed by subject, by title, by product names, by the names of people in the news, and by authors. Under each of those categories, the most recent articles are listed first. The *National Newspaper Index,* a similar index for national newspapers, indexes the most recent five years of the *New York Times, Wall Street Journal, Christian Science Monitor, Washington Post,* and *Los Angeles Times.* The microfilms for both these indexes are already loaded into two separate microfilm-readers that sit side by side on a table in the library, and all you have to do is turn on the machine and press the fast-wind or the slow-wind button to get to that part of the alphabetical listing that has what you are interested in.

Two of the computerized databases that you may find on-line in your local library are *Newsearch* (Belmont, CA: Information Access Corporation) and *Nexis* (Dayton, OH: Mead Data Central). The first of these, for instance, indexes some 400 magazines, 300 trade journals, 5 national newspapers, 700 law journals, and 700 business and management journals. To gain access to this vast reservoir of

B

reference material, you may have to pay a fee, ranging from a few dollars to hundreds of dollars, depending on the number of minutes the search takes and the number of items printed out on the hard copy you are given. At present, this expensive resource is used mainly by graduate students, faculty, and funded researchers, but in order to gather a bibliography in a hurry on certain subjects, you might find it worth the cost to resort to this electronic reference tool. But in order to save yourself a lot of money, you would do well to seek the help of a librarian in the reference department.

ABSTRACTS

After compiling your list of potentially useful books and articles, you might be able to save yourself some wasted motions by consulting the appropriate *collection of abstracts.* By reading a 150–200-word abstract of any of the books and articles on your list, you should be able to tell whether that book or article contains information pertinent to your paper. Most of the scholarly fields now publish annual collections of abstracts of books and articles published during the previous year. The sciences have been publishing abstracts for a number of years, and recently the humanities have begun to publish annual abstracts. You can also use the collection of abstracts as a bibliographical source, since every abstract is headed with the name of the author, the title, and the publication information of the text being summarized.

THE CARD CATALOGUE

The card catalogue—the rows of file-drawers or, increasingly, the terminals which can call up their computerized equivalents—is a valuable resource. Not only does it indicate whether the library has the particular book or periodical you are seeking and where in the library stacks the book or periodical can be found, but it is also another resource for compiling a bibliography for a research project. A library usually has at least three cards in the files for a single book—an *author* card (usually called the "main entry" card), a *title* card, and one or more *subject* cards. **It is the subject cards that give you the best leads on books pertinent to your research project.** Under the appropriate subject heading will be grouped all the books that the library has on a particular subject. You can discover the "appropriate subject heading" from looking at the Library of Congress card for a book that you *know* is pertinent to your study, because on every Library of Congress card, one or more subject headings are suggested for a book.

Most libraries buy the printed cards prepared by a staff of classification experts at the Library of Congress in Washington, D.C. The Library of Congress (abbreviated L.C.) cards carry a lot of information. On page 170, three Library of Congress cards are displayed for a particular book, and the various parts of the card are tagged with letters of the alphabet. The interpretation of those various lettered parts is found on page 171.

When you are compiling a bibliography for your research project, **the most important information for you to copy down from the L.C. card is the author, title, publication information, and call number of the book.** Of that information, the item most crucial for your gaining access to the book is the **call number**. That call number helps either you or the librarian to find the exact spot on the shelf where the book is stored.

You should also be aware of another service that the

B

G

    355
    DAY   The Day after midnight: the effects of nuclear war/edited by
        Michael Riordan; based on a report by the Office of Technology
        Assessment.—Palo Alto, Calif.: Cheshire Books; New York:
        Distributed in by Kampmann & Co., ©1982.

H — ATOMIC WARFARE

    355
    DAY   The Day after midnight: the effects of nuclear war/edited by
        Michael Riordan; based on a report by the Office of Technology
        Assessment.—Palo Alto, Calif.: Cheshire Books; New York:
        Distributed in by Kampmann & Co., ©1982.

        143 p.: ill.; 26 cm.

        Based on: The effects of nuclear war. Washington:
    Congress of the U.S., Office of Technology Assessment, 1979.

A — Riordan, Michael (editor)

B — 355
      DAY   The Day after midnight: the effects of nuclear war/edited by
C   Michael Riordan; based on a report by the Office of Technology
        Assessment.—Palo Alto, Calif.: Cheshire Books; New York:
        Distributed in by Kampmann & Co., ©1982.

D — 143 p.: ill.; 26 cm.

        Based on: The effects of nuclear war. Washington:
    Congress of the U.S., Office of Technology Assessment, 1979.
        Bibliography: p. 130-132.—Includes index.
        $8.00: pbk.
        ISBN: 0-917352-11-4 (pbk.)

E — 1. Atomic warfare I. Riordan, Michael (editor) II. United States.
    Congress. Office of Technology Assessment. The effects of
    nuclear war

F — 018A   82-9538
                               BUR OAK

B

card catalogue and the computer-accessing system can provide. Most of the time when you are faced with the task of
writing a research paper, you do not know the authors and
the titles of pertinent books. You can discover pertinent

A. The **name of the author** (last name first). This *author* card or *main entry card* will be found in the card catalogue in one of the drawers for the letter **R**.

B. The **call number of the book**, typed in by the library staff. This is the number you must copy down if you want to find the book yourself in the stacks or if you want one of the library clerks to get the book for you.

C. The **title of the book and publication information** about the book (i.e., the book is based on a study done for Congress by the U.S. Office of Technology Assessment in 1979).

D. This entry supplies information about the **physical makeup of the book**: there are 143 pages; there are illustrations; and the book is 26 centimeters in height.

E. This entry suggests **other headings** under which the book can be filed.

F. Technical information supplied for the use of the library staff.

G. The **title of the book**. If you knew the title of the book but didn't know the author, you could find the book by looking for this title card in the card catalogue.

H. A **subject heading for the book**, typed in block capitals by the library staff. Note in **E** after the number 1 that *Atomic Warfare* is the first subject heading suggested by the Library of Congress staff.

B

books by consulting the card catalogue or the computer under a subject heading that covers the topic of your research. But the key to discovering a list of books that would be useful for your research is getting the right subject heading. Looking for books under the wrong subject heading might yield the wrong kinds of books or no books at all.

The most helpful reference guide for finding the right subject heading is the two-volume *Library of Congress Subject Headings,* copies of which are readily available in almost every university or public library. Say that you were assigned to do a research paper on the history of parochial schools in the United States and wanted to find what books the university library had on the subject. Before consulting the card catalogue or the computer under the heading of "parochial schools," you would be well advised to look for that heading in one of the alphabetically arranged volumes of *Library of Congress Subject Headings.* There you would discover that "parochial schools" is not one of the recommended headings but that the recommended heading for the library's holdings on the topic is "church schools." Also under this heading in the book, you would find some *See also* references to related subjects, like "church and education," "private schools," and "religious education." By consulting the card catalogue or the computer under one of those headings, you would get a list of all the books in that library on the subject of church-related schools.

C Compiling a Bibliography

In compiling a bibliography—that is, your selected list of the relevant books and articles that you discovered by consulting the appropriate reference sources in the library—you should make a separate 3" × 5" card for each item. Each of these cards should contain the following information (see sample cards on p. 174): (1) the call number of the book or of the bound periodical in which you found the article; (2) the name of the author or editor; (3) the title of the book or article (and, in the case of the article, the title of the magazine or journal in which the article was published); (4) the publication information for the book (the place of publication, the name of the publisher, and the publication date) or the publication information for the article (the volume number of the magazine or journal in which the article appeared, the date of the issue of that magazine or journal, and the first and last page number of the article—e.g., 341–358); (5) some kind of notation—e.g., a subject heading or an explanatory sentence—that will help you later on in quickly identifying the particular area of your study where this book or article fits in.

In filling out these bibliography cards, you should observe this guiding principle: the information recorded on this card should be so complete and accurate that you would never have to go back to the book or the periodical to get or to check any information about it.

If you have been conscientious about gathering pertinent material for your research, you will have a much longer list of books and articles than you need or than you can handle. You will have to trim your list to manageable proportions. That trimming will involve you in some kind of evaluation of the available sources. Here are some criteria that will help you select the most useful and reliable sources: **(1)** the *date* of the book or article (for many studies, usually the later the date of the source, the more useful or reliable the information will be); **(2)** the *reputation* of the author (if you cannot yourself judge the relative authoritativeness of the author, you can consult biographical reference works or reviews of the book or citation indexes); **(3)** the *status* of the publisher or of the periodical (in every field of study, you soon develop a sense for those publishers and periodicals that have acquired a reputation for publishing thorough and reliable scholarship); **(4)** the degree of *pertinence* to your study (even a cursory examination of the available books and articles will often reveal that some of them are more relevant for your purposes than others are).

Here are two sample bibliography cards:

353.6

POTTER, CHARLES FRANCIS

<u>DAYS</u> <u>OF</u> <u>SHAME</u>

NEW YORK: COWARD, 1965
109-110.

(FULL DEVELOPMENT OF ARMY - McCARTHY CONTROVERSY)

070.92

WHITE, THEODORE H.

<u>IN</u> <u>SEARCH</u> <u>OF</u> <u>HISTORY</u>: <u>A</u> <u>PERSONAL</u> <u>ADVENTURE</u>

NEW YORK: HARPER, 1978
395-396.

(LONG - TERM RESULTS OF
McCARTHY ATTACK ON
FOREIGN SERVICE OFFICERS)

ISBN NO.
0-06-014599-4

In each instance the works were written ten to twenty years after the event—long enough to provide some historical perspective **(1)**. Each author carries a measure of authority (Potter was a U.S. Senator in the 1950s and Theodore White is a recognized journalist and historian) **(2)**. Both Coward McCann and HarperCollins are old, reputable publishing houses **(3)**. Pertinence to your study **(4)** then will help you to evaluate these two sources. If your subject is "McCarthyism" and you want to limit your discussion to its *immediate* impact on the military, the Potter book will likely be the better source. If, on the other hand, you want to examine the *long-term* results of the McCarthy era, particularly as it affected military and foreign policy, the White book will better suit your needs.

D   Notes

GATHERING NOTES

If you do enough research, you will eventually develop a system of gathering notes that works best for you. Some people, for instance, just scribble their notes on full sheets of paper or in spiral notebooks. Others record their notes and quotations on 3" × 5" or 4" × 6" cards—*one* note or quotation to a card. The advantage of recording notes on separate cards is that later you can select and arrange the cards to suit the order in which you are going to use them in your paper. It is considerably more difficult to select and arrange notes if they are written out, one after the other, on full sheets of paper. You could, of course, cut out notes from the full sheets, but that activity involves an extra step.

Each notecard should be self-contained—that is, it should contain all the information you would need to document that material properly if you used it in your paper. A notecard is self-contained if you never have to go back to the original source to recover any bit of information about the note. So each notecard should include the following:

1. The particular information you wish to record.

2. Your own shorthand system of referring to the source of the information—for example, the author's last name or a short version of the title—and the page(s) on which the information appears.

3. An indication of whether the note is a summary, a paraphrase, or a direct quotation.

(See the sample notecard on p. 179.)

ACCURACY IN NOTES

Whenever you are transmitting information that you have appropriated from others, you must be scrupulously careful about the accuracy of that information. The question of accuracy is complicated by considerations of whether the material you are transmitting represents a *summary* or a *paraphrase* or a *direct quotation*. If you are transmitting the material in the form of a direct quotation, that quotation must be reproduced exactly as it appeared in the original source. You must not inadvertently add or omit or misspell any words. If you deliberately add words to a direct quotation, you must put those words in square brackets:

> The President said, "He [William Bennett] significantly changed the direction in which NEH [National Endowment for the Humanities] was headed that year [1985]."

If you deliberately omit words from a direct quotation, you must use ellipsis periods to signal the omission:

> The authors of the report say, "Blending may seem simple to an adult who already knows how to read, but . . . it is a difficult step for many children."

If a word was misspelled in the original source, you must reproduce that misspelling in the quotation and signal that the misspelling is not yours by putting *sic* (thus) in square brackets:

> "That is the most flattering complement *[sic]* I have ever received," Professor James said in a letter to the editor.

(See *Ellipsis Periods* and *Square Brackets* on pp. 184–185.)

Accuracy is a more relative matter when you transmit appropriated information in the form of a paraphrase or a summary. What paraphrase and summary have in common is that they represent someone's attempt to render in one's own words information gathered from some outside source. The difference between a paraphrase and a summary is that a paraphrase tends to be a translation of something said in a few sentences, whereas a summary tends to be a translation of something said over several paragraphs or pages. We can objectively judge the accuracy of a direct quotation by checking to see whether the quotation is a verbatim transcription of the original words, but our judgment about the accuracy of a paraphrase or a summary is bound to be more subjective and therefore relative.

Here is a direct quotation from Thomas Babington Macaulay's essay-review of Leopold von Ranke's classic *Ecclesiastical and Political History of the Popes of Rome During the Sixteenth and Seventeenth Centuries* (1840) and five attempts to paraphrase a part of, or to summarize the whole of, this passage:

> During the eighteenth century, the influence of the Church of Rome was constantly on the decline. Unbelief made extensive conquests in all the Catholic countries of Europe and in some countries obtained a complete ascendancy. The Papacy was at length brought so low as to be an object of derision to infidels and of pity rather than of hatred to Protestants. During the nineteenth century, this fallen Church has been gradually

D

rising from her depressed state and reconquering her old dominion. No person who calmly reflects on what, within the last few years, has passed in Spain, in Italy, in South America, in Ireland, in the Netherlands, in Prussia, even in France, can doubt that the power of this Church over the hearts and minds of men is now greater far than it was when the Encyclopaedia and the Philosophical Dictionary appeared.

1. Macaulay maintains that the influence of the Catholic Church was greater in the nineteenth century than at any other time in its history.

2. During the 1700s, according to Thomas B. Macaulay, the influence of the Catholic Church was constantly on the decline.

3. The Roman Papacy, Macaulay avers, is despised by infidels and hated by Protestants.

4. During the eighteenth century, skepticism, Macaulay says, increased in all the Catholic countries of Europe.

5. Thomas Babington Macaulay's thesis is that although the influence of the Roman Catholic Church declined during the eighteenth century, that Church regained its power in Europe during the nineteenth century.

Sentence 1 is an inaccurate paraphrase of the last sentence of the quotation from Macaulay, for what Macaulay said in that final sentence is that the influence of the Catholic Church was greater now in the nineteenth century than it was in the eighteenth century, when the *Encyclopaedia* and the *Philosophical Dictionary* were published.

Sentence 2 is a fairly accurate paraphrase of the first sentence of the original, but the wording and the structure of that paraphrase are so close to the original that this sentence could be regarded as an instance of plagiarism. (See *Plagiarism*, p. 182.)

Sentence 3 is a slightly inaccurate paraphrase of Macaulay's third sentence, because, in relation to the original sentence, it states a half-truth: The Papacy was derided by infidels but, according to Macaulay, only during the eighteenth century, and while the Papacy may have been hated by Protestants at an earlier time, it was pitied rather than hated in the eighteenth century. In short, the paraphrase is misleading.

If the word *skepticism* can be regarded as a synonym for Macaulay's *unbelief,* sentence 4 is an accurate paraphrase of the second sentence of the quotation.

Sentence 5 is an accurate summary of the main point of the quotation from Macaulay.

Note the varying degrees of inaccuracy that we have observed in the five translations.

Sample self-contained notecard:

010.92   McCARTHYISM - KOREAN & VIETNAM WARS

WHITE, THEODORE H.
IN SEARCH OF HISTORY: A PERSONAL ADVENTURE
NEW YORK: HARPER, 1978. 395-396

WHITE SAYS THAT OUR INABILITY TO DEAL EFFECTIVELY WITH ASIAN COUNTRIES DURING THE 50s AND 60s (KOREA & VIETNAM) WAS THE RESULT OF THE LOSS OF A GENERATION OF EXPERIENCED AND DEDICATED FOREIGN SERVICE OFFICERS WHO HAD BEEN DISPERSED TO OTHER POSTS OR PURGED COMPLETELY.
(PARAPHRASED - ITALICS ADDED)

D

Another method of compiling bibliography and notecards is to keep two sets. One set of cards should contain all of the information needed to compile the *Works Cited* at the end of your paper. The other set, keyed to the author and pages in the upper left-hand corner and the subject heading in the upper right-hand corner, is used to record verbatim, summarized, or paraphrased notes.

Verbatim:

POTTER 109-110   McCARTHY-MURROW

"HE SWUNG WILDLY AGAIN AT EDWARD MURROW. HE HAD DISCOVERED THAT IN 1935, MURROW HAD BEEN ON THE NATIONAL ADVISORY COUNCIL OF THE INSTITUTE OF INTERNATIONAL EDUCATION, AN AGENCY WHICH HAD HELPED TO BRING THREE HUNDRED PROFESSORS TO /110/ SAFETY FROM AXIS COUNTRIES AND WHICH ADMINISTERED STUDENT EXCHANGE PROGRAMS BETWEEN THE UNITED STATES AND SEVENTY-FOUR OTHER COUNTRIES. HERE, JOE POINTED OUT, ON A BOOKLET PRINTED NINETEEN YEARS BEFORE, WAS THE DREADFUL TRUTH ABOUT MURROW. THE WORD "MOSCOW" WAS PRINTED RIGHT ON THE COVER OF THE SAME BOOK THAT DISPLAYED A PHOTOGRAPH OF MURROW"

(ITALICS ADDED)

D

Note that quotation marks have been used to indicate that it is a direct quotation, that the page number between slashes (/110/) shows where the quotation went over from one page to the next, and that the notation "italics added" shows that it was the researcher, not the author, who italicized the words.

Paraphrased:

WHITE 395-396

MCCARTHYISM—
KOREAN & VIETNAM WARS

WHITE SAYS THAT OUR INABILITY TO DEAL
EFFECTIVELY WITH ASIAN COUNTRIES DURING
THE 50s AND 60s (KOREA AND VIETNAM) WAS
THE RESULT OF THE LOSS OF A GENERATION OF
EXPERIENCED AND DEDICATED FOREIGN SERVICE
OFFICERS WHO HAD BEEN DISPERSED TO OTHER
POSTS OR PURGED COMPLETELY.

(ITAL. ADDED)

E   Incorporating Sources

WHAT NEEDS TO BE DOCUMENTED?

As you draft your paper, you will have to develop a sense
for what needs to be documented. Here are some guidelines to help you:

1. Any direct quotation should be followed by a citation of the
   source. Be sure to enclose the quotation in quotation marks.

2. Paraphrased material may or may not need to be followed by a
   parenthetical citation of the source. If, for instance, the fact or
   information that you report in your own words is *generally
   known* by people knowledgeable on the subject, you probably
   would not have to document that paraphrased material. For
   example, if you were writing a research paper on the assassina-
   tion of Abraham Lincoln, you ordinarily would not have to
   document your statement that John Wilkes Booth shot Lincoln

E

in Ford's Theater in Washington in April of 1865, because that historical fact is common knowledge. But if one of the arguments in your paper concerned the *exact time of the day* when he was shot, you would have to document your statement that Lincoln was shot at 8:40 P.M. on the evening of April 14, 1865. When, however, you cannot resolve your doubt about whether paraphrased material needs to be documented, document it.

3. When you are summarizing, in your own words, a great deal of information that you have gathered from your reading, you can be spared having to document several sentences in that summary by using a *content endnote*. (See the discussion on p. 190 regarding the proper use and format of endnotes.)

PLAGIARISM

If you present as your own words what you have copied from some other author or if you present some paraphrased material without acknowledging the source of the data or information, you are guilty of plagiarism. (See the section on *Accuracy in Notes,* p. 176, for some examples of acceptable and unacceptable paraphrases.) The academic community regards plagiarism as a very serious offense, punishable by a failing grade on the paper or by a failing grade in the course or by dismissal from school. If you value your personal integrity and your status in school, you should resist the temptation to engage in this kind of intellectual dishonesty. For what needs to be documented in a paper, see the three guidelines presented in the previous section.

KEEP QUOTATIONS TO A MINIMUM

A research paper should not be just a pastiche of long quotations stitched together by an occasional comment or by a transitional sentence by the author of the paper. You should use your own words as much as possible, and when you do quote, you should keep the quotation brief. Often a quoted phrase or sentence will make a point more emphatically than a long quotation. You must learn to look for the phrase or sentence that represents the kernel of the quotation and to use that extract rather than the full quotation. Otherwise, the point you want to make with the quotation may be lost in all the verbiage. You will be more likely to keep your quotations short if you try to work most of them into the framework of your own sentence, like this:

> The *New York Times* claims that the recent increase in enrollments at community colleges across the nation is "the main reason that total enrollment in higher education has not fallen, as educational forecasters expected would happen by now" (Maeroff).

Sometimes, however, when you find it difficult to present the essential point in a short extract, you will have to quote something at greater length. Long quotations (two sentences or more) should be *inset* ten spaces from the left-hand margin, with *no quotation marks enclosing the quotation*, and *triple-spaced* between the long quotation and the rest of the text like this:

```
To support his contention, Carl Sagan cites an

empirical study that was done to determine the

most common varieties of dreams:


          Statistical studies have been made of

          the most common categories of dreams--

          studies which, at least to some extent,

          ought to illuminate the nature of
```

E

dreams. In a survey of the dreams of
college students, the following were,
in order, the five most frequent types:
(1) falling; (2) being pursued or
attacked; (3) attempting repeatedly
and unsuccessfully to perform a task;
(4) various academic learning
experiences; and (5) diverse sexual
experiences (164–165).

ELLIPSIS PERIODS

Ellipsis periods (three spaced periods) are used to indicate
that a word or several words or whole sentences have been
omitted from a direct quotation:

> The president said last week that "the American people . . .
> would not tolerate such violence."

(Note that there is a space between periods; wrong form: ...)

The three spaced periods indicate that a string of words
has been omitted. To show the deletion of whole sentences,
insert the ellipsis, while retaining the original punctuation
(the period immediately after the word *context* below is the
usual period that marks the end of a sentence):

> These results have no connection with any genuine attempt to
> use words in a normally expected context. . . . A similar ar-
> tificial monstrosity could be contrived by jumbling together
> inappropriate metaphors.

Usually there is no need to put ellipsis periods at the

beginning or end of a quotation, because the reader knows that the quotation has been extracted from a larger context. Reserve ellipsis periods for indicating omissions *within* quotations. Take care that such omissions do not destroy the original meaning or intent of the passage.

SQUARE BRACKETS

Square brackets are used to enclose anything that the author of the research paper inserts into a direct quotation:

> About this tendency to indulge in scatological language, H. A. Taine wrote, "He [Swift] drags poetry not only through the mud, but into the filth; he rolls in it like a raging madman, he enthrones himself in it, and bespatters all passers-by."

> The Senator was emphatic in stating his reaction to the measure: "This action by HEW [Health, Education, and Welfare] will definitely not reverse the downward spiral [of prices and wages] that has plagued us for the last eight months."

> We find this entry in the Japanese admiral's diary: "Promptly at 8:32 on Sunday morning of December 6 [*sic*], 1941, I dispatched the first wave of bombers for the raid on Perl Harber [*sic*]."

*(**Sic** is a Latin adverb meaning "thus," "in this manner," and is used to let the reader know that the error in logic or fact or grammar or spelling in the quotation has been copied exactly as it was in the original source. It is italicized because it is a foreign word.)*

If your typewriter does not have keys that make square brackets, you will have to draw the brackets with a pen after you remove the paper from the typewriter, and so you should leave spaces for the brackets.

E

F   Documenting Sources—MLA System

In the second edition of the *MLA Handbook for Writers of Research Papers,* edited by Joseph Gibaldi and Walter S. Achtert and published in the autumn of 1984, and in the subsequently published *The MLA Style Manual* (1985), the Modern Language Association (MLA) presented its radical change in the style of documenting research papers that had been standard for most books and journals in the humanities since the first edition of the *MLA Style Sheet* appeared in 1951. Instead of indicating the source of quotations and citations in footnotes or in endnotes, the MLA system now uses a parenthetical style of documentation, much like the APA system (see the details of the APA system on pp. 205–207). The MLA Committee on Research Activities believes that this new system of documentation is characterized by "precision, accuracy, economy, consistency, clarity, and comprehensibility" and that it will help to bridge the gap that had existed between the documentation system of the humanities and that of other disciplines.

The two substantive consequences of the change are (1) that footnotes or endnotes are no longer used to indicate the source of quotations and citations that appear in the text of a research paper and (2) that all researched essays—even those published in professional journals—carry a bibliography of all the works cited in the paper. The essence of the new style of documentation is that some kind of lead-in in the text tells the reader that a quotation or citation or allusion is about to be presented and a brief reference presented in parentheses tells the reader where

F

to look in the *Works Cited* page for full biblio
information about the source of that quotation, ci
allusion.

There are other, mainly mechanical, changes in
MLA style of documentation:

1. Arabic numerals, rather than Roman numerals, are used to indicate the volume numbers of books as well as journals. (Roman numerals, however, will still be used (a) to identify a person in a series—e.g., Henry VIII, Pope John XXIII; (b) to cite the pages in the preliminary section of a book—e.g., viii, xiv; (c) to designate some conventional references—e.g., (*Hamlet* IV ii 25–30, *PL* VI 160–2).

2. The abbreviations **p.** (for *page*) and **pp.** (for *pages*) have been eliminated before page numbers, even when no volume number is given.

3. The abbreviations **l.** (for *line*) and **ll.** (for *lines*) have been eliminated before line numbers.

4. The comma after the title of a journal has been eliminated— e.g., *German Quarterly* 34 (1961): 78–82.

5. A colon separates the volume number (and date) from the page number–e.g., 97 (1962): 318–24 or 2:57.

6. For journals that begin each issue with page 1, the volume number *and* issue number are given—e.g., *American-German Review* 20.4 (1954): 9–10. Sometimes, however, it might be desirable to give the month or the season also—e.g., 58.2 (May 1964): 113–4, or 30.3 (Winter 1945): 87.

7. The place of publication is given as it is spelled on the title page or the copyright page. Therefore, sometimes the foreign name of a city rather than the Anglicized name is given in the bibliographical reference—e.g., *Praha* for Prague, *München* for Munich, *Braunschweig* for Brunswick. (In some cases, however, it might be useful to give the Anglicized spelling of the city in brackets—e.g., *Köln* [Cologne].

F

MODEL PARENTHETICAL CITATIONS

The general principle governing parenthetical documentation is that only as much additional information should be given within the parentheses as is necessary to enable the reader to determine the source of the quotation or citation or allusion. For instance, if the lead-in for a quotation in the text supplies the name of the author and if only one work by that author is given on the *Works Cited* page at the end of the paper, only the page number of the quoted works needs to be given in the parentheses. (See the first of the following examples.)

1. **Author Cited in the Lead-in:**

   Travis says that jazz was incubated in Chicago, even though it was not conceived there (8–9).

2. **Author Not Cited in the Lead-in:**

   Jazz was incubated in Chicago, even though it was not conceived there (Travis 8–9).

3. **Two or Three Authors:**

   Logan and Cohen credit the Niagara Movement with being the first successful organized effort to voice the Negro protest in the twentieth century (164)

4. **More Than Three Authors:**

   "Popular sovereignty" meant that settlers could vote for or against slavery at the first meeting of their territorial legislature (Divine et al. 384–85).

5. **Unknown Authorship:**

   In architecture, integration of the arts should complement the architectural forms and enhance the total environment (Conrad Schmitt Studios).

F

6. Two or More Works by the Same Author:

"Hollywood, or a segment of it at least, was becoming increasingly active on the question of civil rights" (Baldwin, *No Name in the Street* 132).

"Some argue that a people cannot have a future until they accept their past" (Baldwin, *The Fire Next Time* 95).

[**Note:** Shortened versions of titles are acceptable—e.g., *No Name* or *Fire*.]

7. Multivolume Work:

Other and more serious problems than transportation were raised by the westward movement after the war (Morison & Commager 1:441).

8. Government Document or Corporate Author:

The Commission on Law Enforcement and Administration of Justice concluded that there is far more crime than is ever reported (v).

9. A Novel:

Melville's narrator describes Captain Ahab as having "an eternal anguish in his face . . ." (90; ch. 28).

F

10. A Poem:

An example of personification is Tennyson's "broad stream in his banks complaining . . ."(*Shalott* 3.120).

11. A Play:

They were, in fact, "a pair of star-crossed lovers" (*Romeo and Juliet* Prologue.6).

12. An Interview:

When questioned about how wise it is for actors to take work doing commercials, my friend expressed no concern that the practice would jeopardize his career (Lordan).

13. Citing an Entire Work:

(When citing an entire work, rather than just a part of the work, it is preferred that the author's name be included in the text—*not* in a parenthetical reference.)

Fleming uses this kind of approach throughout *Arts & Ideas*.

ENDNOTES/FOOTNOTES

In cases where several sources are cited and it is necessary to indicate volume numbers, page numbers, multiple authors, etc., an endnote (or footnote) should be used. Clearly, the following citation would be intrusive and disruptive in your text:

(Holmes 118–22; Sims and Bates 1:233–34; Whitfield iv–vii; Ray 97; Scott et al. 512–14)

A superscript numeral is used in the text to direct the reader to the page titled **Notes** at the end of the paper or to a footnote that appears at the bottom of the page.

Two or more works can be included in a single parenthetical reference simply by separating them with a semicolon:

(Keplar 616; Alvarez 97–99)

F

G   The *Works Cited* Page—MLA Style

GENERAL INSTRUCTIONS

In a research paper, the bibliography is placed at the end of the paper. It is here that the researcher provides full information about all the sources used in the paper. Start the list on a new page and proceed as follows:

1. The heading **Bibliography** or **Works Cited** should be centered, one inch down from the top of the page.
2. Double-space between the heading and the first entry.
3. Begin the first entry flush with the left-hand margin. If an entry requires more than one line, indent all subsequent lines five spaces from the left margin.
4. Double-space between *and* within entries and continue the list for as many pages as necessary.

Alphabetize the entries by the author's last name or, if the work is anonymous, according to the first letter of the first significant word in the title. For example, *A Handbook of Korea* is alphabetized under "H."

MODEL *WORKS CITED* ENTRIES

1. A Single Book by a Single Author:
Seki, Hozen. *The Great Natural Way.* New York: American Buddhist Academy, 1976.

2. A Single Book by More Than One Author:
Baran, Paul A., and Paul M. Sweezy. *Monopoly Capital: An Essay on American Economic and Social Order.* New York: Monthly Review P, 1966.

3. A Book of More Than One Volume:
Hays, William Lee, and Robert L. Winkler. *Statistics: Probability, Inference, and Decision.* 2 vols. New York: Holt, 1970.

G

4. A Book Edited by One or More Editors:

Coats, Alfred W., and Ross M. Robertson, eds. *Essays in American Economic History.* London: Edward Arnold, 1969.

Smith, David Nicol, ed. *The Letters of Jonathan Swift to Charles Ford.* Oxford: Clarendon P, 1935.

5. An Essay or a Chapter by an Author in an Edited Collection:

Svaglic, Martin J. "Classical Rhetoric and Victorian Prose." *The Art of Victorian Prose.* Ed. George Levine and William Madden. New York: Oxford UP, 1968. 268–88.

6. A New Edition of a Book:

Doughty, Oswald. *A Victorian Romantic, Dante Gabriel Rossetti.* 2nd ed. London: Oxford UP, 1960.

7. A Book That Is Part of a Series:

Heytesbury, William. *Medieval Logic and the Rise of Mathematical Physics.* University of Wisconsin Publications in Medieval Science. No. 3. Madison: U of Wisconsin P, 1956.

8. A Book in a Paperback Series:

Wilson, Edmund. *To the Finland Station.* Anchor Books. Garden City, NY: Doubleday, 1955.

9. A Translation:

Dostoevsky, Fyodor. *Crime and Punishment.* Constance Garnet, trans. New York: Heritage, 1938.

10. A Signed and an Unsigned Article from an Encyclopedia:

Ewing, J. A. "Steam-Engine and Other Heat-Engines." *Encyclopaedia Britannica.* 9th ed. 1980.

"Dwarfed Trees." *Encyclopedia Americana.* 1948.

11. An Article from a Journal:

Adkins, Nelson. "Emerson and the Bardic Tradition." *Publications of the Modern Language Association* 72 (1948): 662–67.

12. An Article in a Popular Magazine:

Levin, Robert J. "Sex, Morality, and Society." *Saturday Review* 9 July 1966. 29–30.

13. A Signed and an Unsigned Article in a Newspaper:

Van Matre, Lynn. "Evergreen Rockers: '60s stars built to last." *Chicago Tribune* 12 Jan. 1986, final ed.: 13:20.

"Panel says FDA not doing its job." *Chicago Tribune* 13 Jan. 1986, Chicagoland ed.: 8.

14. A Signed Book Review:

Dalbor, John B. Rev. of *Meaning and Mind: A Study in the Psychology of Language*, by Robert F. Terwilliger. *Philosophy & Rhetoric* 5 (1972): 60–61.

15. A Government Booklet or Pamphlet:

United States. Social Security Administration. *Aid to Families with Dependent Children: 1973 Recipient Characteristics Study*. Publication No. (SSA). 77–11777. June 1975.

16. A Personal Letter or Interview:

Glenn, Senator John. Letter to the author. 20 June 1983.

Herrens, Malcolm B. Telephone interview. 3 February 1980.

17. A Recording or Jacket Notes:

Seeger, Pete, and Arlo Guthrie. "Joe Hill." *Together in Concert*. Warner, HR 3120, 1975.

18. A Film, a Radio Program, or a Television Program:

Tootsie. With Dustin Hoffman, Jessica Lange, and Teri Garr. Writ. Don McGuire and Larry Gelbart. Dir. Sydney Pollack. A Mirage/Punch Production. Columbia, 1982.

H Model Research Paper—MLA Style

Tracey Smith Perdue   Perdue 1

Professor Engstrom

ENG 111.01

February 22, 1989

The Stratosphere and Chlorofluorocarbons:

A Recipe for Disaster

Imagine for just a moment living in an environment like
that of prehistoric earth. Lush tropical forests, dense and
thick, tangle their way across the surface. Temperatures, warm
and balmy, bring stifling humidity to blanket the land. To
some, this scene may seem like paradise. But during this time,
other parts of the world would be converted to desert. Higher
temperatures and shifting weather patterns would foretell of
drought and widespread crop failure (Gribbin 97–100).
Multitudes of people would be uprooted, left with no choice but
to become environmental refugees (Lemonick "Heat" 37).
Unfortunately, this imagined scene is not far from reality.
According to the scientific community, a worldwide climatic
warming could occur by the twenty-first century. If the
stratosphere continues to be destroyed at current levels,
climatic warming will determine mankind's ultimate fate

(Gribbin 97). Indeed, as Noel Grove says, this warming "has the potential to alter life on this planet" (512).

To understand how our environment is being altered, we must first understand the complex chemistry of the atmosphere. There are many chemicals that contribute to the destruction of the ozone. Everything from volcanic eruptions to vehicle emissions can be held responsible ("Pollution" 86). Undoubtedly, one of the major contributors to this destruction is chlorofluorocarbons (CFCs). Alone, F—11 and F—12, just two of the many CFC family chemicals, account for 29 percent of the greenhouse effect (Gribbin 94). In fact, CFCs in general are much more efficient (20,000 times more efficient!) at generating the greenhouse effect than the dreaded carbon dioxide we hear so much about (Lemonick "Danger" 42). But first, a word about the ozone and how it works.

For our purposes, the ozone is defined as the second layer of the atmosphere. It surrounds our globe in a band somewhere between seven and twenty—five miles above the surface of the earth. To the experts, it is the stratosphere. Ozone comprises three atoms of oxygen. This ozone oxygen (O_3) is created when regular oxygen (O_2) from lower bands of the atmosphere is swept upward. At the higher altitudes, the O_2 oxygen is exposed to

H

solar radiation from the sun. When this radiation occurs, some of the O_2 molecules are broken apart. These single atoms are then free to attach themselves to other O_2 molecules, thus forming O_3 or ozone (Gribbin 2-4).

The advantage to having a stratospheric ozone layer is that it repels ultraviolet radiation emanating from the sun. This layer acts like a shield, deflecting dangerous rays and protecting all life forms ("Pollution" 86). The ozone also works like insulation by retaining heat and weather in the lower layer of the atmosphere and allowing the global mean-temperature to remain steady at 59° F (Gribbin 86). To understand how this protective layer is destroyed by CFCs, we now look at their chemical composition.

CFCs are a family of chemicals with atoms of chlorine, fluorine, and carbon in varying quantities. They were originally developed for refrigeration purposes but quickly became widely used in various industries because of their chemical characteristics. In general, CFCs are nonflammable, nontoxic, cheap to produce, and chemically very stable. These characteristics made them ideal for a whole range of applications. From the blowing agent in foam industries to the cleaning solvent in the semiconductor computer age, CFCs were

thought to be the perfect chemical solution (Gribbin 40-1).
But it is these very same characteristics that make CFCs deadly
to the ozone (Lemonick "Danger" 42).

CFCs, like O_2, are swept into the stratosphere by wind
currents. All CFCs eventually reach these higher altitudes
because their chemical stability prevents them from being
broken apart at lower levels. Furthermore, they are not washed
from the sky by rain. In fact, F-11 remains in the atmosphere
for approximately seventy-five years, and F-12 remains for an
astounding 110 years (Gribbin 44-7).

Once CFCs reach the stratosphere, they are broken apart by
the same radiation that breaks apart the O_2 molecule. The irony
is that once a chlorine atom is released in this manner, it is
then free to break apart ozone molecules, a fracturing that it
proceeds to do with military efficiency (Gribbin 46-8).
Chlorine is so destructive that Sherry Rowland of the
University of California at Irvine estimates that one atom of
chlorine can obliterate 100,000 molecules of ozone before it
becomes stable once again and falls from the sky (Gribbin 59).
This link between CFCs and the depletion of the ozone is
evident. As scientists have discovered, wherever ozone levels
have dropped, high amounts of CFC chemical concentrations have

H

been found ("Ozone" 12). The frightening reality is that
virtually all CFCs ever released are still present in, and are
still inflicting damage on, the atmosphere (Gribbin 47).

The effect of billions of tons of CFCs in the stratosphere
is twofold. First, CFCs destroy the ozone's reflecting
capability. Because CFCs break apart O_3 molecules, there is
less ozone to block the sun's rays. Hence, more ultraviolet
radiation now reaches the earth's surface (Gribbin 17).
Second, because CFC molecules act better as insulation, the
heat radiated from the earth is trapped near the surface. This
trapped heat causes global warming and generates the greenhouse
effect (Lemonick "Danger" 42). But we will look at each of
these problems individually.

As more ultraviolet radiation (UV) reaches the earth,
human beings can expect to be at greater health risk. Recently,
Congress was told that "the steady increase in skin cancer of
recent years is caused not by more sunbathing but by a thinning
of the ozone" ("Very Air" 93). In fact, the Environmental
Protection Agency (EPA) estimates that for every 1 percent
decrease in the total ozone, there is a 5 percent increase in
skin cancer in the United States alone (Gribbin 17). What is
even more terrifying is the effect UV—B, a particular band of

ultraviolet radiation, has on DNA, the very building blocks of life. The National Research Council, in a report to the EPA, concluded that damage to DNA, which is the primary target of UV–B in animal cells, would most likely result in mutagenesis. The report suggests that damage to DNA would ultimately cause cell mutation, neoplastic transformation, or death. None of these effects sound very beneficial for human beings (Committee 6). However, as stated earlier, this damage to DNA is not the only problem confronting the world.

The entrapment of heat in lower levels of the atmosphere may be by far the most disastrous of consequences. This containment of heat is referred to as the greenhouse effect, and as noted earlier, CFCs are certainly more effective at trapping heat than normal ozone molecules. One problem associated with the warming trend would be the melting of the polar ice caps. This melting would in turn raise the ocean levels by as much as fifteen to twenty feet (Grove 515), and low–lying areas such as Bangladesh and Holland would most probably end up submerged ("Very Air" 92). Likewise, many areas in the United States would also feel the pressure of rising water levels. Southern Louisiana, which is at present losing gulf–front property at a rate of one acre every sixteen

H

minutes, would most definitely be affected (Elmer-DeWitt 70).
Still other problems caused by global warming would be just as
serious.

Scientists have suggested another consequence of the
greenhouse effect: changes in climatic weather patterns. On a
worldwide scale, droughts, floods, hurricanes, and heat waves
could become increasingly common should the global mean-
temperature rise by just 3° F. The magnitude of human suffering
from these natural disasters would be unprecedented (Lemonick
"Heat" 36-7). Unfortunately, these possibilities are already
becoming reality. Since 1850 the global mean-temperature has
risen by 1° F, and it appears that the temperature will continue
to rise at an alarming rate well into the next century ("Very
Air"). As stated by James Hansen, head of NASA's Goddard
Institute for Space Studies, "The evidence is pretty strong
that the greenhouse effect is here" (Lemonick "Heat" 36).

Just how extensive is this problem? As reported by the
Goddard Institute, the ozone layer remained relatively steady
from 1978, the first year Goddard began tracking ozone
depletion, to 1983. During this seven-year span, the total
amount of ozone declined by 4 percent (Gribbin 145).
Coincidentally, 1984 was the year that the largest amount of

CFCs had been released worldwide since 1977, an estimated billion pounds (Siwolop 113). If early calculations can be trusted, scientists predict the ozone will have diminished by 20 to 40 percent by the first part of the next century (Gribbin 48).

If there is any indication of what the future holds, that indication can be seen over the South Pole right now. Here the ozone has been depleted by as much as 60 percent, leaving a gaping hole in the stratosphere each spring (Brown 191). As stated in "Nature" in 1987, scientific evidence "leave[s] little doubt that the development of the Antarctic ozone hole involves chlorine chemistry as a direct and prominent feature" (Gribbin 123). As good as scientists are at evaluating the problems of CFC contamination, they do not have the power to stop the flow of chemicals into our atmosphere. These solutions will not come easily or cheaply, but we must begin to overcome obstacles.

The biggest barrier to effective solutions is the fact that this problem is a worldwide issue. According to Senator Albert Gore, "Solutions require international cooperation on a scale that is totally unprecedented in history" (Gore 66). Because two-thirds of all CFC emissions are produced by

countries other than the United States, cooperation on a
worldwide level is the only choice that mankind has to
permanently halt this destruction ("Ozone" 12). Although
Montreal Protocol, a treaty signed by twenty-four nations to
reduce CFC production 35 percent by the year 2000, was an
attempt at addressing the problem, it may be too little too
late (Lemonick "Danger" 42). According to environmentalists,
in 1987 an 85 percent reduction was needed immediately to
prevent additional buildup of CFCs in the stratosphere
("Ozone" 12).

The gap between what is needed and what industrial
nations, pressured by manufacturers, are likely to adopt is
wide indeed. U.S. manufacturers, wanting neither regulation by
the government nor the expensive responsibility of safe
emission levels, are putting heavy pressure on congressional
leaders ("Ozone" 12). Their tactics appear to have been
successful during the Reagan Era because regulation of CFCs has
virtually come to a halt since the beginning of the 1980s
(Gribbin 60). Because the United States is slow to embrace
effective regulations, other countries are reluctant as well.
Japan, which produces 11 percent of the world's total CFC
output, may refuse to participate in the Montreal Protocol
altogether ("Ozone" 12). And taking into account the Third
World's ambition of achieving economic development, we find it

unlikely that this part of the world will curb CFC use at the expense of industrialization. And still other obstacles exist. Everything from lack of funds for alternative research to disbelief in the severity of the problem contributes to further delays in action.

The greenhouse effect is a legacy which the industrialized world has forged in just 100 years. In this brief span of time, we have managed to contaminate the atmosphere to a level never before seen by modern man. If we continue to spew chemicals, like chlorofluorocarbons, into the air, we will undoubtedly achieve a global warming of a magnitude not seen on earth in two million years (Gribbin 97). If we do not take action now, we will see this dramatic change in our lifetime. Indeed, this global warming is a frightening legacy. The question is "Will we stop it in time?"

WORKS CITED

Brown, Linda J. "Facts about the Ozone." Good Housekeeping
    Aug. 1988: 191.
Committee on Chemistry and Physics of Ozone Depletion et al.
    Causes and Effects of Stratospheric Ozone Depletion: An
    Update. Washington: National Academy, 1982.
Elmer-DeWitt, Phillip (Reported by J. Madeline Nash).
    "Preparing for the Worst." Time 2 Jan. 1989: 70-1.

Gore, Albert. "What is Wrong with Us?" Time 2 Jan. 1989: 66.

Gribbin, John. The Hole in the Sky: Man's Threat to the Ozone
    Layer. New York: Bantam, 1988.

Grove, Noel. "Air: An Atmosphere of Uncertainty." National
    Geographic Apr. 1988: 502-37.

Lemonick, Michael D. "Deadly Danger in a Spray Can." Time
    2 Jan. 1989: 42.

————. "Feeling the Heat." Time 2 Jan. 1989: 36-9.

"The Ozone Problem: A Global Pact to Patch the Roof." US News &
    World Report 21 Sept. 1987: 12.

"Pollution: Taking the Air in Antarctica." The Economist
    28 June 1986: 86.

Siwolop, Sana. "The Ozone Layer is Shrinking Faster than
    Expected." Business Week 16 June 1986: 113.

"The Very Air." The Economist 16 May 1987: 92-3.

H

I The APA System of Documentation

Just as the MLA system of documentation, illustrated in the previous section, is predominant in the humanities, the American Psychological Association (APA) system is predominant in such fields as psychology, education, psycholinguistics, and many of the social sciences. Over 200 scholarly journals in the United States now prescribe the APA style of documentation. The highlights of this system will be presented here; for a fuller treatment, consult the readily available paperback edition of *Publication Manual of the American Psychological Association,* 3rd ed. Washington, D.C.: American Psychological Association, 1983.

The principal difference between the MLA and the APA systems is that the MLA in-text and parenthetical citations feature the name of the author and the location of the information; the APA citations feature the name of the author, the date, and the location. The date is featured in scientific writing for the obvious reason that a researcher must present the most up-to-date information that is available.

Here is how the first reference to a book would be documented, first in the MLA style and then in the APA style. (Note that the APA in the parentheses retains the abbreviations "p." and "pp." and puts a comma between the author's name and the date of publication.)

1. **Author Cited in the Lead-in:**

    MLA Tracy defended the "big-bang" theory (234).

    APA Tracy (1985) defended the "big-bang" theory (p. 234).

2. **Author Not Cited in the Lead-in:**

    MLA The "big-bang" theory can be defended (Tracy 234).

    APA The "big-bang" theory can be defended (Tracy, 1985, p. 234).

Readers who wanted fuller information about the work cited in the parenthetical reference could turn to the list of references at the end of the paper. There, in an alphabetical listing, the Tracy work would be entered in doublespaced typescript as follows:

Tracy, Arnold. (1985). *New theories on the origins of the universe.* New York: Downey.

VARIATIONS ON THE BASIC APA STYLE OF DOCUMENTATION

1. If a whole work is being referred to, only the author's last name and the date of the work are given in parentheses.

   A recent study has confirmed that twelve-year-olds grow at an amazingly rapid rate (Swanson, 1969).

2. A page number or a chapter number is supplied only if part of a work is being referred to. Quotations always demand the addition of a page number.

   The committee boldly declared that "morality could not be enforced, but it could be bought" (Dawson, 1975, p. 105).

3. Any information supplied in the text itself need not be repeated in the parentheses.

   Anderson (1948) found that only middle-class Europeans disdained our cultural values.

   In 1965, Miller professed his fervent admiration of our admissions policy.

4. If a work has two authors, both authors should be cited each time a reference is made to that particular text. If a work has

three or more authors, all the authors should be cited the first time, but subsequently only the name of the first author followed by **et al.** needs to be given.

The circulation of false rumors poisoned the environment of that conference (Getty & Howard, 1979).

The overall effect of the smear tactics was a marked decline in voter registrations (Abraham, Davis, & Keppler, 1952).

In three successive national elections, voters from Slavic neighborhoods showed a 72% turnout (Abraham et al., 1952, pp. 324–327).

5. If several works are cited at the same point in the text, the works should be arranged alphabetically according to the last name of the first author and should be separated with semicolons.

All the studies of the problem agree that the proposed remedy is worse than the malady (Brown & Turkell, 1964; Firkins, 1960; Howells, 1949; Jackson, Miller, & Naylor, undated; Kameron, in press).

6. If several works by the same author are cited in the same reference, the works are distinguished by the publication dates, arranged in chronological order and separated with commas. Two or more works published by the same author in the same year are distinguished by the letters **a, b, c,** etc., added to the repeated date. In such chronological listings, works "in press" are always listed last.

A consistent view on this point has been repeatedly expressed by the Canadian member of the Commission (Holden, 1959, 1965, 1970, 1971a, 1971b, 1976).

7. If no author is given for a work, two or three words from another part of the entry (usually from the title) should be used to refer to the work.

The voter's apathy was decried in the final spring meeting of the city council ("The Gradual Decline," 1976).

LIST OF REFERENCES

The *References* page appended to a paper that observes the APA style is comparable to, and yet different from, the *Works Cited* page in a paper that observes the MLA style. Both systems give full bibliographic information about the works cited in the body of the writing, and both systems arrange the entries alphabetically according to the last name of the author. In both systems, the names of the authors are inverted (surname first), but in the APA system, only the initials of first and middle names are given, and when there are two or more authors for a work, the names of *all* the authors are inverted.

The conventions of sequence, punctuation, and capitalization in the APA style for the *References* section can most easily be illustrated with examples.

1. A Book by a Single Author:

Luria, A. R. (1973). The working brain: An introduction to neuropsychology. London: Penguin.

Note that the title of the book is underlined but that only the first word of the title and the first word following the colon in the title are capitalized. (Any proper nouns in a title would also be capitalized; see the following example.) The three main parts of an entry—author, title, and publication data—are separated with periods. Also note that you should leave *two* spaces after the colon separating the place of publication and the name of the publisher.

2. A Book by Several Authors:

Koslin, S., Koslin, B. L., Pargament, R., & Pendelton, S. (1975). An evaluation of fifth grade reading programs in ten New York City Community School Districts, 1973–1974. New York: Riverside Research Institute.

Note that the names of all the authors are inverted, that the names are separated with commas, and that an ampersand (**&**) is put before the last name in the series (even when there are only two names; see the following example.)

3. An Article in an Edited Collection:

Bobrow, D. G., & Norman, D. A. (1975). Some principles of memory schemata. In D. G. Bobrow & A. M. Collins (Eds.), Representation and understanding: Studies in cognitive science. New York: Academic Press.

Note that the title of the article (**Some principles** etc.) is not enclosed in quotation marks and that only the first word of this title is capitalized. (Any proper nouns in the title of the article would, of course, be capitalized.) Note also that the subsequent names of the two editors (**Eds.**) of the collection are not inverted and that there is no comma between the names.

4. An Article in a Journal:

Stahl, A. (1977). The structure of children's compositions: Developmental and ethnic differences. Research in the Teaching of English, 11, 156–163.

Note that all substantive words in the title of the journal are capitalized and that the title of the journal is underlined. Note also that the year comes after the author's name and that the volume number (**11**) is underlined. For a journal that begins the numbering of its pages with page 1 in each issue, the number of the issue should be indicated with an Arabic number following the volume number—**11(3)**.

5. A Book by a Corporate Author:

American Psychological Association. (1966). Standards for educational and psychological tests and manuals. Washington, DC: Author.

I

Books and articles with corporate authors are listed alphabetically according to the first significant word of the entry (here **American**). The word **Author** indicates that the publisher of the work is the same as the group named in the author slot. If, however, the publisher is different from the corporate author, the name of that publisher would be given right after the place of publication.

These five models cover most of the kinds of published material likely to be used in a research paper. For additional models, consult the *Publication Manual of the American Psychological Association* (3rd ed.).

For an illustration of the physical appearance, in typescript, of a research paper and of *References* done according to the APA system of documentation, see the following pages, taken from a 21-page article by Carl Bereiter of the Ontario Institute for Studies in Educaton: "Development in Writing," in *Testing, Teaching and Learning* (Washington, D.C.: National Institute of Education, 1979), pp. 146–166. This article was later reprinted in L. W. Gregg and E. R. Steinberg, eds., *Cognitive Processes in Writing* (Hillsdale, N.J.: Erlbaum, 1979).

I

DEVELOPMENT IN WRITING

Carl Bereiter

Although there is a substantial body of data on the development of writing skills, it has not seemed to have much implication for instruction. Reviews of writing research from an educational perspective have given scant attention to it (Blount, 1973; Braddock, Lloyd-Jones, & Schoer, 1963; Lyman, 1929; West, 1967). Generally speaking, developmental research has educational significance only when there is a conceptual apparatus linking it with questions of practical significance.

Almost all of the data on writing development consist of frequency counts—words per communication unit, incidence of different kinds of dependent clauses, frequency of different types of writing at different ages, and so on. The conceptual frameworks used for interpreting these data have come largely from linguistics (e.g., Hunt, 1965; Loban, 1976; O'Donnell, Griffin, & Norris, 1967). However informative these analyses might be to the student of language development, they are disappointing from an educational point of view. The variables they look at seem unrelated to commonly held purposes of writing instruction (Nystrand, 1977).

The purpose of this paper is to synthesize findings on the growth of writing skills within what may be called an "applied cognitive-developmental" framework. Key issues within an applied cognitive-developmental framework are the cognitive strategies children use and how these are adapted to their limited information processing capacities (Case, 1975, 1978; Klahr & Wallace, 1976; Scardamalia, in press). Although this paper will not deal with instructional implications, it will become evident that the issues considered within an applied cognitive-developmental framework are relevant to such concerns of writing instruction as fluency, coherence, correctness, sense of audience, style, and thought content.

Students' writing will undoubtedly reflect their overall language development (Loban, 1976; O'Donnell et a., 1967) and also their level of cognitive development (Collis & . . .

References

Allen, R. L. (1972). English grammars and English grammar. New York: Scribner's.

Blount, N. S. Research on teaching literature, language, and composition. (1973). In R. M. W. Travers (Ed.), Second handbook of research on teaching. Chicago: Rand McNally.

Braddock, R., Lloyd–Jones, R., & Schoer, L. (1963). Research in written composition. Champaign, IL: National Council of Teachers of English.

Case, R. (1975). Gearing the demands of instruction to the developmental capacities of the learner. Review of Educational Research, 45(1), 59–87.

Case, R. (1978). Implications of developmental psychology for the design of effective instruction. In A. M. Lesgold, J. W. Pellegrino, S. D. Fokemma, & R. Glaser (Eds.), Cognitive psychology and instruction. Plenum, NY: Division of Plenum Publishing Corporation.

Collis, K. F., & Biggs, J. B. (undated). Classroom examples of cognitive development phenomena. ERDC Funded Project 7/41, University of Newcastle.

I

Gleason, H. A., Jr. (1965). Linguistics and English grammar. New York: Holt, Rinehart & Winston.

Hunt, K. W. (1965). Grammatical structures written at three grade levels. Champaign, IL: National Council of Teachers of English. (Research Report No. 3.)

Klahr, D., & Wallace, J. G. (1976). Cognitive development: An information-processing view. Hillsdale, NJ: Erlbaum.

Loban, W. (1963). The language of elementary school children. Urbana, IL: National Council of Teachers of English. (Research Report No. 1.)

Loban, W. (1966). Problems in oral English. Urbana, IL: National Council of Teachers of English. (Research Report No. 5.)

Loban, W. (1976). Language development: Kindergarten through grade twelve. Urbana, IL: National Council of Teachers of English. (Research Report No. 18.)

Long, R. B. (1961). The sentence and its parts: A grammar of contemporary English. Chicago: University of Chicago Press.

Writing
19

Lyman, R. (1929). Summary of investigations relating to grammar, language, and composition. Chicago: University of Chicago. (Supplementary educational monographs, No. 36, published in conjunction with The School Review and The Elementary School Journal.)

Nystrand, M. (1977). Assessing written communication competence: A textual cognition model. Toronto, Canada: The Ontario Institute for Studies in Education. (ERIC Document Reproduction Service No. ED 133 732.)

O'Donnell, R. C., Griffin, W. J., & Norris, R. C. (1967). Syntax of kindergarten and elementary school children: A transformational analysis. Champaign, IL: National Council of Teachers of English. (Research Report No. 8.)

Scardamalia, M. (in press). How children cope with the cognitive demands of writing. In C. H. Frederiksen, M. S. Whiteman, & J. F. Dominic (Eds.), Writing: The nature, development, and teaching of written communicaton.

West, W. W. (1967). Written composition. Review of Educational Research. 37(2), 159–167.

J   Other Documentation Systems

Most of the scholarly disciplines specify the style of documentation that they prefer, and when you begin to major in one of those disciplines, you will be expected to use that style of documentation in the research papers or articles that you write. In the masthead of professional journals, the editor usually indicates what system of documentation authors should observe in the articles they submit for consideration.

Here is a list of the style manuals for a few of the disciplines:

Council of Biology Editors. Style Manual Committee. CBE Style Manual: A Guide for Authors, Editors, and Publishers in the Biological Sciences. 5th ed. Bethesda: Council of Biology Editors. 1983.

American Chemical Society. Handbook for Authors of Papers in American Chemical Society Publications. Washington: American Chemical Society, 1978.

American Mathematical Society. A Manual for Authors of Mathematical Papers. 7th ed. Providence: American Mathematical Society, 1980.

International Steering Committee of Medical Editors. "Uniform Requirements for Manuscripts Submitted to Biomedical Journals." Annals of Internal Medicine 90 (January 1979): 95–99.

American Institute of Physics. Publications Board. Style Manual for Guidance in the Preparation of Papers. 3rd ed. New York: American Institute of Physics, 1978.

FORMS FOR LETTERS

GENERAL INSTRUCTIONS

The one type of writing that most people engage in after leaving school is letter-writing. You will almost certainly write letters to parents, friends, and acquaintances, and you may have to write letters in connection with your job. Occasionally, you may feel compelled to write a letter to the editor of a newspaper or magazine, and sometimes you may write more formal letters to institutions or officials for such purposes as applying for a job, requesting information or service, or seeking redress of some grievance. Although you do not have to be much concerned about the niceties of form when you are writing to intimate friends, you would be well advised to observe the conventions of form and etiquette in letters addressed to people that you do not know well enough to call by their first names.

Format of Familiar Letter

Letters written to acquaintances are commonly referred to as *familiar letters*. Although usually "anything goes" in letters to acquaintances, you should keep in mind that even the most intimate acquaintance is flattered if the author of the letter observes certain amenities of form. Here is a list of the conventions for the familiar letter.

(a) Familiar letters may be written on lined or unlined paper of any size.

(b) Familiar letters may be handwritten and may be written on both sides of the sheet of paper.

(c) The author of the letter usually puts his or her address and the date at the right-hand side of the heading but does not, as in a business letter, put at the left-hand side of the heading the name and address of the person to whom the letter is addressed.

(d) Depending on the degree of intimacy with the addressee, you may use salutations like these: **Dear Mom, Dear Jim, Dear Julie, Dear Ms. Worth**. The salutation is often followed by a comma rather than the more formal colon.

(e) The body of the letter may be written in indented paragraphs, single- or double-spaced.

(f) Depending on the degree of intimacy with the addressee, you may use complimentary closes like these: **Sincerely, Cordially, Affectionately, Yours, Much love, Fondly, As ever**.

(g) Depending on the degree of intimacy with the addressee, you may sign your full name or just a first name or a nickname.

Format of Business Letter

Formal letters addressed to organizations or customers or professionals or executives are commonly called *business letters*. The form of business letters is more strictly prescribed than the form of familiar letters. Models for a business letter appear on pp. 221 and 223. Here is a list of the conventions for the business letter:

(a) Business letters are written on 8½ × 11 unlined paper or on 8½ × 11 paper with a printed letterhead.

(b) Business letters must be typewritten, single-spaced, on one side of the paper only.

(c) In the sample business letter that is typed on printed letterhead stationery (p. 223), the so-called *full block* format of formal business letters is illustrated. Note that in this format, everything—date, address, greeting, text, complimentary close—begins at the left-hand margin. Compare this format with the *semiblock* format of the sample business letter that is typed on plain white paper (p. 221). All the other directions about format (**d, e, f, g, h, i, j**) apply to both kinds of formal business letters.

(d) Flush with the left-hand margin and in single-spaced block form, type the name and address of the person or the organization to whom the letter is written. (The same form will be used in addressing the envelope.)

(e) Two spaces below this inside address and flush with the left-hand margin, type the salutation, followed by a colon. In addressing an organization rather than a specific person in that organization, use salutations like **Dear Sir** or **Gentlemen** or **Dear Madam** or **Ladies**. If you know the name of the person, you should use the last name, prefaced with **Mr.** or **Miss** or **Mrs.** or, if uncertain about the marital status of a woman, **Ms.**—e.g., **Dear Mr. Toler, Dear Miss Cameron, Dear Mrs. Nakamura, Dear Ms. Ingrao**. Women who feel that marital status should be no more specified in their own case than in that of a man (for whom **Mr.** serves, irrespective of whether he is married) prefer **Ms.** to **Mrs.** and **Miss**. The plural of **Mr.** is **Messrs.**; the plural of **Mrs.** or **Ms.** is **Mmes.**; the plural of **Miss** is **Misses**. Professional titles may also be used in the salutation: **Dear Professor Newman, Dear Dr. Marton**. (*Webster's New Collegiate Dic-*

tionary carries an extensive list of the forms of address for various dignitaries [judges, clergy, legislators, etc.].)

(f) The body of the letter should be single-spaced, except for double-spacing between paragraphs. Paragraphs are not indented but start flush with the left-hand margin.

(g) The usual complimentary closes for business letters are these: **Sincerely yours, Yours truly, Very truly yours**. The complimentary close is followed by a comma.

(h) Type your name about three or four spaces below the complimentary close. The typed name should not be prefaced with a professional title (**Dr.**, **Rev**.) nor followed with a designation of academic degrees (**M.A.**, **Ph.D**.), but below the typed name, you may indicate your official capacity (**President**, **Director of Personnel**, **Managing Editor**). You should sign your name in the space between the complimentary close and the typed name.

(i) If one or more copies of the letter are being sent to others, that fact should be indicated with a notation like the following in the lower left-hand side of the page (**cc** is the abbreviation of **carbon copy**):
cc: **Mary Hunter**
     Robert Allison

(j) If the letter was dictated to, and typed by, a secretary, that fact should be indicated by a notation like the following, which is typed flush with the left-hand margin and below the signature (the writer's initials are given in capital letters, the secretary's in lowercase): **WLT/cs** or **WLT:cs**.

See the following models for the text and envelope of the two styles of business letters.

Semiblock

239 Riverside Road
Columbus, OH 43210
January 5, 1991

Mr. Thomas J. Weiss
Manager, Survey Division
Acme Engineering Company, Inc.
5868 Fanshawe Drive
Omaha, NB 68131

Dear Mr. Weiss:

Mr. Robert Miller, sales representative of the Rushmore Caterpillar
Company of Columbus and a long-time friend of my father, told me that
when he saw you at a convention in Chicago recently, you indicated
you would have two or three temporary positions open this summer in
your division. Mr. Miller kindly offered to write you about me, but
he urged me to write also.

By June, I will have completed my junior year in the Department of
Civil Engineering at Ohio State University. Not only do I need to
work this summer to finance my final year of college, but I also need
to get some practical experience in surveying tracts on a large road-
building project such as your company is now engaged in. After checking with several of the highway contractors in this area, I have
learned that all of them have already hired their quota of engineering
students for next summer.

For the last three summers, I have worked for the Worley Building
Contractors of Columbus as a carpenter's helper and as a cement-
finisher. Mr. Albert Michaels, my foreman for the last three summers,
has indicated that he would write a letter of reference for me, if
you want one. He understands why I want to get some experience in
surveying this summer, but he told me that I would have priority for
a summertime job with Worley if I wanted it.

Among my instructors in civil engineering, the two men who know me best
are Dr. Theodore Sloan, who says that he knows you, and Mr. A. M.
Slater. Currently, I have a 3.2 quality-point average in all my subjects,
but I have straight A's in all my engineering courses. For the last two
quarters, I have worked as a laboratory assistant for Professor Sloan.

I am anxious to get experience in my future profession, and I am quite
willing to establish temporary residence in Omaha during the summer.
I own a four-cylinder sub-compact car that I could use to travel to
the job site each day. I am in good health, and I would be available
to work for long hours and at odd hours during the summer months. If
you want any letters of recommendation from any of the men named in
my letter, please let me know.

Sincerely yours,

Oscar Jerman

Oscar Jerman

cc: Robert Miller

Business letter typed on plain, unlined paper

Addressed Business-size Envelope

Oscar Jerman
239 Riverside Road
Columbus, OH 43210

Mr. Thomas J. Weiss
Manager, Survey Division
Acme Engineering Company, Inc.
5868 Fanshawe Drive
Omaha, NB 68131

Full Block

EDUCATIONAL ASSOCIATES, INC.

PHONE 815-727-9452

SUITE 400, RIALTO SQUARE BUILDING • 5 EAST VAN BUREN STREET • JOLIET, IL 60431

February 23, 1991

Dr. John A. Whitney
Superintendent
Garden Grove High School
Garden Grove, IL 60488

Dear Dr. Whitney:

The week that my staff and I spent on your campus was an unusually
productive one. It is rare to find both the level of awareness
and the commitment to finding solutions to problems that is
present in the Garden Grove school district.

A report of our findings and recommendations will be available
on March 15. I think we should meet as soon as possible after
that date to review the material it will contain. Perhaps we
can also talk then about the best way to distribute the report.
Some administrators prefer to present our reports themselves--
others find it more appropriate for a member of our staff to
do it. You know better than we do what is best for your district.

I will be in Washington, D.C. from March 13 through March 16.
I will be available at the time most convenient for you after
that.

Please extend our thanks and appreciation to your faculty and
staff, students, parents, and school board members for their
cooperation during our visit to Garden Grove.

Sincerely yours,

Kathleen W. Bolden

Kathleen W. Bolden
President
Educational Associates, Inc.

KWB/ig

cc: Richard K. Rapp
     President, Board of Education
     Garden Grove High School

Business letter on letterhead stationery

Letterhead Business Envelope

Dr. John A. Whitney
Superintendent
Garden Grove High School
Garden Grove, IL 60488

EDUCATIONAL ASSOCIATES, INC.
SUITE 400, RIALTO SQUARE BUILDING
5 EAST VAN BUREN STREET
JOLIET, IL 60431

THE TWO-LETTER POSTAL ABBREVIATIONS

On the following page is the U.S. Postal Service list of two-letter abbreviations of the fifty states, the District of Columbia, and outlying areas. These abbreviations should be set down in capital letters without a period and should be followed by the appropriate five- or nine-digit ZIP code—for example, New York, NY 10022–5299.

Alabama	**AL**		Montana	**MT**
Alaska	**AK**		Nebraska	**NE**
Arizona	**AZ**		Nevada	**NV**
Arkansas	**AR**		New Hampshire	**NH**
California	**CA**		New Jersey	**NJ**
Colorado	**CO**		New Mexico	**NM**
Connecticut	**CT**		New York	**NY**
Delaware	**DE**		North Carolina	**NC**
District of Columbia	**DC**		North Dakota	**ND**
Florida	**FL**		Ohio	**OH**
Georgia	**GA**		Oklahoma	**OK**
Guam	**GU**		Oregon	**OR**
Hawaii	**HI**		Pennsylvania	**PA**
Idaho	**ID**		Puerto Rico	**PR**
Illinois	**IL**		Rhode Island	**RI**
Indiana	**IN**		South Carolina	**SC**
Iowa	**IA**		South Dakota	**SD**
Kansas	**KS**		Tennessee	**TN**
Kentucky	**KY**		Texas	**TX**
Louisiana	**LA**		Utah	**UT**
Maine	**ME**		Vermont	**VT**
Maryland	**MD**		Virgin Islands	**VI**
Massachusetts	**MA**		Virginia	**VA**
Michigan	**MI**		Washington	**WA**
Minnesota	**MN**		West Virginia	**WV**
Mississippi	**MS**		Wisconsin	**WI**
Missouri	**MO**		Wyoming	**WY**

A RÉSUMÉ

A résumé (pronounced *REZ-oo-may*) is also referred to by, and sometimes even labeled with, the Latin terms *curriculum vitae* (the course of one's life) or *vita brevis* (a short life) or simply *vita*. Whatever name it bears, this document presents, usually on one or two pages and in the form of a list, a summary of an applicant's job objective, education, work experience, personal experiences, extracurricular activities, achievements, honors, etc. Sent out with a cover letter that is addressed to a specific person in the company, the résumé is intended to introduce the applicant to a potential employer and to elicit a request for further information about the applicant and ultimately for an interview.

Under such headings as *Education, Work Experience,* and *Extracurricular Activities,* the items are usually listed in reverse chronological order, starting with the most recent and ending with the earliest. The items that the applicant chooses to list should be pertinent to the kind of job being sought. The cover letter that accompanies the résumé should call attention to those items that are especially pertinent to the particular job that is being applied for.

The résumé and the cover letter should be neatly, flawlessly, and attractively typed on good heavy bond paper. The physical appearance alone of these documents could make a crucial impression on the reader. You cannot afford to be sloppy or careless in preparing these documents. Remember that you are trying to sell yourself and the service you have to offer. So in listing your assets and achievements, do not misrepresent yourself, either by exaggerating or by downplaying your merits. Do not brag; let the facts speak for themselves. For example, if you mention that you have a four-year Grade Point Average of 3.8, you do not have to boast that you have been an excellent student.

The résumé usually mentions that letters of reference and transcripts of academic work are available upon request. In the case of students who are applying for a job, the résumé sometimes gives the address of the school's placement office where the interested employer can write for the applicant's dossier, which is a collection of such documents as transcripts, letters of reference, and samples of one's writing. If your résumé and cover letter move the potential employer to write for your dossier, you will have reached an important stage in the process of applying for a job. The next important step is to gain an invitation to a face-to-face interview.

A Résumé

MARY LEE HALE

<u>Home Address</u>   <u>Campus Address</u>
11 Top St.   45 Race St.
Newark, OH 43055   Columbus, OH 43210
513/267-4819   614/422-6866

JOB OBJECTIVE

To obtain a position in an advertising or marketing capacity, with an
emphasis in either product development, sales, or promotional strategy.

EDUCATIONAL HIGHLIGHTS

B.S. degree in Advertising, College of Communications, Ohio State
     University, Columbus, Ohio--May, 1986
Equivalent to a minor in marketing
Cumulative grade point average: 3.48; major field grade point average: 3.6

RELEVANT ADVERTISING AND MARKETING COURSES

Introduction to Advertising   Advertising Media
Creative Strategy and Tactics   Sales Writing
Advertising in Contemporary Society   Marketing Research
Advertising Management   Marketing Behavior
Advertising Research   Operations Research

PRIOR WORK EXPERIENCE

Sept. 1985–   McBride's Pharmacy, Columbus, Ohio
present   Cashier

May–August   Industrial Techtonics, Weymouth, Ohio
1985   Market Development Coordinator
                     --effected sales through personal calls and correspondence
                     --created a company brochure
                     --developed new customer contacts through correspondence

August 1984–   Campus Daily News/Digest, Columbus, Ohio
March 1985   Advertising manager and sales representative
                     --conceptualized and executed advertising plans
                     --persisted in efforts to maximize revenues through
                        generation of new clients and revitalization of
                        stagnated accounts
                     --motivated sales representatives to become more efficient

August 1982–   Rosalee Apparel, Inc., Columbus, Ohio
April 1984   Sales Clerk
                     --introduced to the challenge of sales through the
                        commission system
                     --developed the ability to relate to and meet the needs of
                        a wide variety of people

EXTRACURRICULAR ACTIVITIES

Dorm Vice-President   Little Sister--Zeta Beta Tau Fraternity
Volunteer Project--Blood Drive   Intramural softball and volleyball

        REFERENCES   INTERESTS

   Available upon request   Skiing, tennis, needlepoint

GLOSSARY OF USAGE

Many of the entries here deal with pairs of words that writers often confuse because the words look alike or sound alike. Ascertain the distinction between these confusing pairs and then invent your own memorizing device to help you make the right choice in a particular case. In all cases of disputed usage, the most conservative position on that usage is presented so that you can decide whether you want to run the risk of alienating that segment of your readers who subscribe to the conservative position on matters of language use.

accept, except. When writers don't keep their wits about them, they occasionally get these two words mixed up and inadvertently use the wrong word. Most of the time, **except** is used as a preposition, in the sense of "with the exclusion of, other than, but": *Everyone was dressed up except me*. The alternative prepositional form **excepting** should be used only in negative constructions: *Waiters must report all income to the IRS, not excepting tips*. Sometimes **except** is used as a conjunction, followed by **that**: *She would have called, except that she could not find his telephone number*. The word **accept** may never be used as a preposition—although in a careless moment, a writer might enscribe this sentence: *They approved of all the candidates accept him*. The word **accept** is a verb, in the sense of "to receive, to take in": *She graciously accepted his apology*. On the rare occasions when **except** is used as a verb, in the sense of "to exclude, to leave out, to omit," writers sometimes use the wrong verb, as in this sentence: *My brother was accepted from the dean's list because his grades were not high enough.* (Write instead, *My brother was excepted from the dean's list because his grades were not high enough.*) All in all, **accept** and **except** are tricky words. Be careful.

adverse, averse. Both of these words are adjectives that are used in the sense of opposition, but from different perspectives. The opposition expressed by the word **averse** is always from the subject's point of view, as in *The pastor was averse to their whispering in church* (that is, the pastor was opposed to their whispering in church). The opposition expressed by the word **adverse** exists outside the subject, as in *She overcame the adverse circumstances.* The idiomatic preposition to use with **averse** is **to**.

advice, advise. Adopt some mnemonic device to help you remember that **advice** is the noun form and that **advise** is the verb form. *She accepted his advice* (noun). *The doctors advised him to stop smoking* (verb). Pronouncing the two words may help you get the right spelling.

affect, effect. The noun form is almost always **effect** (*The effect of that usage was to alienate the purists*). The wrong choices are usually made when writers use the verb. The verb **effect** means "to bring about, to accomplish" (*The prisoner effected his escape by picking a lock*). The verb **affect** means "to influence" (*The weather affected her moods*).

allusion, illusion. Think of **allusion** as meaning "indirect reference" (*He made an allusion to her parents*). Think of **illusion** as meaning "a deceptive impression: (*He continued to entertain this illusion about her ancestry*).

alot, a lot. This locution should always be written as two words (*A lot of the natives lost faith in the government*).

already, all ready. **All ready** is an adjective, meaning "completely prepared" (*By 3:00, the team was all ready to go*). **Already** is an adverb, meaning "by this time, previously" (*By 3:00, the team had already left the gymnasium*).

alright, allright, all right. **All right** is the only correct way to write this expression (*He told his mother that he was all right*).

altogether, all together. **Altogether** is the adverb form, in the sense of "completely" (*She was not altogether happy with the present*). **All together** is the adjective form, in the sense of "collectively" (*The students were all together in their loyalty to the team*).

among. See **between**.

amount of, number of. When you are speaking of masses or bulks, use **amount of** (*They bought a large amount of sugar*). When you are speaking of persons or things that can be counted one by one, use **number of** (*They bought a large number of cookies*). See **fewer, less**.

any more. The adverb **any more** should not be used in positive statements, as in these instances: *They were surprised that you visit us any more* and *The television stations have good programs any more*. But this adverb may be used in negative statements, as in the following instances: *They were surprised that you do not visit us any more* and *The television stations don't have good programs any more*; and in questions, as in this instance: *Do you write to your parents any more?* Most arbiters of usage recommend that this adverb be written as two words, but at least two of the reputable dictionaries authorize the single-word form, **anymore**.

as, like. See **like, as**.

because of. See **due to**.

beside, besides. Both of these words are used as prepositions, but **beside** means "at the side of" (*They built a cabin beside a lake*), and **besides** means "in addition to" (*They bought a jacket besides a pair of boots*).

between. The conservative position is that **between** should be used only when two persons or things are involved (*They made a choice between the Democrat and the Republican*). Use **among** when three or more persons or things are involved (*Faced with a half dozen choices, he could not decide among them*).

can't help but. Conservatives regard this expression as an instance of a double negative (**can't** and **but**). This sentence, *She can't help but love him*, they would rewrite as *She can't help loving him*.

center around. One frequently sees and hears an expression such as *His interest centered around his work*. This expression seems to violate the basic metaphor from which it derives. How can something center **around** something else? Say instead *His interest centered **on** his work* or *His interest centered **upon** his work*.

complement, compliment. Writers frequently mix up these like-sounding words. **Complement**, both as a noun and as a verb, carries the notion of "something that completes or adds to" (*Traveling complements the education we get in school*); **compliment**, both as a noun and as a verb, carries the notion of "an expression of praise" (*He grinned from ear to ear whenever his teacher paid him a compliment*). Devise your own mnemonic device to help you write the right word for what you intend to say.

comprise. **Comprise** is a tricky word. This verb means "to include." So it is correct to write *The state comprises seventeen counties.* It is incorrect to write *Seventeen counties comprise the state* or *The state is comprised of seventeen counties.* The formula is "The whole comprises the parts. The parts do not comprise the whole." Instead of saying *The state is comprised of seventeen counties,* say *The state is composed of seventeen counties.* Be wary of this tricky word.

continual, continuous. There is a real distinction between these two adjectives. Think of **continual** as referring to something that occurs repeatedly (that is, with interruptions). For instance, a noise that recurred every three or four minutes would be a "continual noise"; a noise that persisted without interruptions for an hour would be a "continuous noise." **Continual** is stop-and-go; **continuous** is an uninterrupted flow.

could of, should of, would of, may of, might of. In the spoken language, these forms sound very much like the correct written forms. In writing, use the correct forms: **could have, should have, would have, may have, might have.** In informal contexts, you may use the accepted contractions, such as **could've, should've, would've.**

data. The word **data,** like the words **criteria, phenomena, media,** is a plural noun and therefore demands the plural form of the demonstrative adjective (*these data, those data*) and the plural form of the verb (*These data present convincing evidence of his guilt. The data were submitted by the committee*).

different from, different than. In British usage, **different than** is more likely to be used than **different from** when a clause follows the expression (*This treatment is different than we expected*). In conservative American usage, **different**

from is preferred to **different than**, whether the expression is followed by a noun phrase (*The British usage is different from the American usage*) or by a noun clause (*This treatment is different from what we expected*).

disinterested, uninterested. Careful writers still make a distinction between these two words. For them, **disinterested** means "unbiased, impartial, objective" (*The mother could not make a disinterested judgment about her son*). **Uninterested**, for them, means "bored, indifferent to" (*The students were obviously uninterested in the lecture*).

due to, because of. Many writers use **due to** and **because of** interchangeably. Some writers, however, observe the conservative distinction between these two expressions: **due to** is an adjectival construction, and **because of** is an adverbial construction. Accordingly, they would always follow any form of the verb **to be** (**is, were, has been**, etc.) with **due to** (*His absence last week was due to illness*); moreover, they would always follow transitive and intransitive verbs with the adverbial construction **because of** (*She missed the party because of illness* and *He failed because of illness*). Sometimes, they might substitute **owing to** or **on account of** for **because of**.

effect. See **affect**.

enthuse, enthused. You will frequently hear people use these words as verbs, as in the sentence *They enthused about the plans for the dance*. Linguists would call this verb form a "back formation" from the noun **enthusiasm** or the adjective **enthusiastic**. Purists frown on this verb form. They would say *They were enthusiastic about the plans for the dance*.

farther, further. Conservatives insist that **farther** is the correct word to use when one is referring to physical distance, as in the sentence *The campers travelled farther than they expected to on that day*. They insist that **further** is the correct word to use in the figurative or abstract sense of additional time, degree, or quantity, as in sentences such as these: *The campers took off without further delay* and *The teacher insisted that they consider the matter further* and *They demanded a further explanation for the delay*. Although no one ever uses **farther** in the abstract or figurative sense (for instance, *They gave the matter farther consideration*), some writers will use **further** where conservatives insist on the use of **farther** (for instance, *That mountain is further away than I thought*). Observe the traditional distinction between **farther** and **further** if you do not want to run the risk of alienating some of your readers.

fewer, less. Use **fewer** with countable items (*That beer has fewer calories in it than the Canadian beer has*). Use **less** when speaking of mass or bulk (*Elmer has less sand in his garden than Andrew does*). See **amount of**, **number of**.

good, well. If you remember that **good** is an adjective and that **well** is an adverb, you won't write *He did good on the exam* or *The car runs good*. Instead, you will write *He did well on the exam* and *The car runs well*. And you will write *She is good about taking her medicine* and *The pie tastes good*.

hopefully. Many people object to the use of **hopefully** in the sense of "it is to be hoped," as in the sentence *Hopefully, we can finish our term papers by the deadline*. If you want to avoid offending those who object to this usage, you will rewrite a sentence like the one above to read *We hope that we can finish our term papers by the deadline*.

human, humans. Those who take a conservative view of language have not yet accepted **human** or **humans** as a noun. They would rewrite *The natives made no distinction* *between animals and humans* in this fashion: *The natives made no distinction between animals and human beings.* In their view, **human** should be used only as an adjective.

imply, infer. There is a definite difference in meaning between these two verbs. **Imply** means to "to hint at, to suggest," as in *She implied that she wouldn't come to his party.* **Infer** means "to deduce, to draw a conclusion from," as in *He inferred from the look on her face that she wouldn't come to his party.*

irregardless. This is one of the "double negatives" (**ir-** and **-less**) that in some people's minds does irreparable damage to the user's reputation as a literate person. If you use the word **regardless**, your reputation for irreproachable literacy will be preserved.

kind of, sort of. Do not use the article **a** or **an** with either of these phrases: *He suffered some kind of a heart attack* and *She got the sort of an ovation that she deserved.* Rewrite these sentences in this way: *He suffered some kind of heart attack* and *She got the sort of ovation that she deserved.* **Kind of** and **sort of** in the sense of "rather" or "somewhat" (*He was kind of annoyed with his teacher*) should be reserved for an informal or a colloquial context.

lend, loan. The conservative position is that **loan** should be used exclusively as a noun (*He took out a loan from the bank*) and that **lend** should be used exclusively as a verb (*The bank lends him the down payment*).

less. See **fewer**.

lie, lay. **Lie** (past tense **lay**, present participle **lying**, past participle **lain**) is an intransitive verb meaning "to rest, to recline," as in *The book is lying on the table* or *The book lay there yesterday* or *It has lain there for three days.* **Lay** (past tense **laid**, present participle **laying**, past participle **laid**) is a transitive verb (that is, it must be followed by an object) meaning "to put down," as in *She is laying the book on the table* or *Yesterday she laid the book on the mantelpiece.*

like, as. Avoid the use of **like** as a subordinating conjunction, as in *At the party, he behaves like he does in church.* Use **like** exclusively as a preposition (*At a party, he behaves like a prude*). **As** is the appropriate subordinating conjunction with clauses (*At a party, he behaves as he does in church*).

likely, liable, apt. Some writers use these words interchangeably: *Their daughter is likely* (or *liable* or *apt*) *to get her way.* Discriminating writers, however, reserve **liable** for an undesirable happening, as in *If he is contradicted, he is liable to lose his temper,* and reserve **likely** for a favorable happening, as in *If he is contradicted, he is likely to smile and shake your hand warmly.* **Liable** is also the word to use in legal contexts, as in *If you don't remove the snow from your sidewalk, you are liable to be fined.* **Apt** is used in the sense of "inclined," as in *It is apt to be foggy here early in the morning,* and also in the sense of "appropriate or suitable," as in *That was an apt remark.*

literally. Originally, **literally** was used as an adverb meaning the opposite of **figuratively.** In recent years, some people have been using the word as an intensifier (*She literally blew her top*). Careful writers still use the word in its original sense of "actually" (*The mother literally washed out her son's mouth with soap*).

loose, lose. These common words look alike but do not sound alike, and they differ in meaning (**loose,** "unfastened"; **lose,** "mislay"). Here is a device to help you remember the difference in meaning. The two *o*'s in **loose** are like marbles dumped out of a can (*The dog broke its leash* *and ran loose in the backyard*). The word **lose** has lost one of its *o*'s (*I always lose my wallet when I go to a carnival*). If this memorizing device does not help you keep the two words straight, invent your own device.

may of, might of. See **could of**.

off of. *My youngest son skinned his nose when he jumped off of the moving carousel.* Using **of** with **off**, as in the previous sentence, is redundant. Say simply *He jumped off the moving carousel.*

O.K. This most distinctively American expression has appeared in various forms in the written medium: **OK, okay, oke, okeh, okey**—among others. But **O.K.** is the prevailing form. This versatile word has been used as a noun (*My boss gave his O.K. to my plan*); as an adjective (*That was an O.K. thing to do* or *He said it was O.K. for me to leave the door unlocked*); as an adverb (*The computer was working O.K. when I left it*); and as an interjection (*O.K., so let's get going*). There is widespread agreement among the arbiters of usage that **O.K.** is acceptable in informal, colloquial contexts. **O.K.** is widely used in written communications in the business world.

past, passed. These words are more sound-alikes than look-alikes. The word with the *-ed* ending is the only one that can be used as a verb (*His car passed mine on the freeway*). The word **past** is versatile: it can be used as a noun (*I recalled my sordid past*); as an adjective (*I recalled the past events*); and as a preposition (*His car sped past mine like a bullet*). But **past** should never be used as a verb, as in this sentence: *His car past mine.*

principal, principle. These words sound alike, but they are spelled differently, and they have different meanings.

Whether used as a noun or as an adjective, **principal** carries the meaning of "chief." The noun form to designate the chief of a high school is **principal**. (Some people use this mnemonic device to guide them in using the right spelling for the chief officer of a high school: "The **principal** is your **pal**"). The adjective that means "chief" is always **principal** (*The principal administrative officer of a high school is the principal*). The word **principle** is used only as a noun and means "rule, law" (*A manufacturer should observe the basic principles of physics*).

quote(s). In formal contexts, use **quotation(s)** instead of the colloquial contraction **quote(s)**.

reason is because. This phrasing constitutes an example of faulty predication (see section **40**). Write *The reason is that . . .*

reason why. This phrasing is redundant. A reason is a *why*. Instead of writing *The reason why I am unhappy is that I lost my wallet*, drop the redundant **why** and write *The reason I am unhappy is that I lost my wallet*.

respectfully, respectively. Choose the correct adverb for what you want to say. **Respectfully** means "with respect" (*She answered the questions very respectfully*). **Respectively** means "the previously mentioned items in the order in which they are listed" (*Mary Sarton, Maria Gonzalez, and Sarah Fowler were the first, second, and third presidents of the Guild, respectively*).

set, sit. **Set**, like **lay**, is a transitive verb (that is, it takes an object, as in *She set the vase down carefully on the table*). **Sit**, like **lie**, is an intransitive verb (that is, it expresses action but action that does not terminate in an object). So you should write *They sit on the porch*, not *They set on the porch*. However, there are a few idioms in which **set** is used as an intransitive verb: *The sun sets* and *A hen sets*. And there are at least two idioms in which **sit** is used as a transitive verb: *She sits herself down* and *A rider sits a horse*.

should of. See **could of**.

so, such. Avoid the use of **so** and **such** as an intensifier, as in sentences such as *She was so happy, It was such a cold day*. If you must use an intensifier, use such adverbs as **very**, **exceedingly**, **unusually** (*She was very happy* and *It was an unusually cold day*). If you use **so** or **such** to modify an adjective, your readers have a right to expect you to complete the structure with a *that*-clause of result (*She was so happy that she clapped her hands for joy* and *It was so cold that we had to clap our hands to keep warm*).

sort of. See **kind of**.

supposed to, used to. Because it is difficult to hear the *-d* when these phrases are spoken, writers sometimes write *He was suppose to arrive yesterday* or *He use to eat here at noon*. Always add the *-d* to these words.

their, there, they're. All three words are pronounced alike. The wrong one is chosen in a particular instance, not because the writer does not know better but becaue the writer has been careless or inattentive. (Is there any of us who has not occasionally used the wrong one of these three words?) Because every literate person knows the different meanings of these three words, we do not have to review those meanings here. Just be careful to use the right word for what you want to say.

try and. In the spoken medium, one frequently hears utterances such as *Try and stay within the white lines if you can*. Purists insist that we write *Try to stay within the white lines if* *you can*. So if we want to be "proper," we should always write **try to** instead of **try and**.

unique. The word **unique** basically means "one of a kind." Purists, therefore, insist that it is just as ridiculous to say *more unique* or *most unique* as it is to say *more perfect* or *most perfect*. It is highly likely that such qualifications of the word **unique** will eventually be acceptable, if they are not already sanctioned by most arbiters of usage. But if you do not want to raise the eyebrows of any of your readers, do not write such sentences as *Their policy is the most unique one in the industry*. What is not debatable is that the article **a**, not **an**, should be used in front of **unique** (*That is a unique policy*).

used to. See **supposed to**.

whose, who's. Since the two words are pronounced alike, it is understandable that writers sometimes make the wrong choice. The word spelled with the apostrophe is the contraction of "who is" (*Who's the principal actor? Who's playing the lead role?*). **Whose** is (1) the interrogative pronoun (*Whose hat is this?*), (2) the possessive case of the relative pronoun **who** (*John is the man whose son died last week*), and (3) an acceptable possessive form of the relative pronoun **which** (*Our flag, whose broad stripes and bright stars we watched through the perilous fight, was gallantly streaming over the ramparts*).

would of. See **could of**.

you. **You** is the second-person personal pronoun, both singular and plural. We all recognize when this pronoun is referring to a definite person, as in *My dear, I am asking you if you will marry me*, or to definite persons, as in *I ask all of you to give me your undivided attention*. What has become questionable usage is the use of the indefinite **you**, as in

Today, you have to be rich in order to survive and *Most doctors agree that if you avoid fatty foods, you will lessen the chance of your having a heart attack.* In those sentences, the **you** is not a real person out there. In those sentences, **you** is being used where careful writers use the indefinite pronoun **one**, as in *Today, one has to be rich in order to survive.* Each writer has to decide whether he or she will adopt the increasingly prevalent practice of using the indefinite **you**.

COMMONLY MISSPELLED WORDS

accept (cf. except)
accidentally
accommodate
acquire
acquaintance
address
all right
already (cf. all ready)
argument
arithmetic
athletics
attendance

beginning
believe
benign
business

cemetery
changeable
chief
choose (cf. chose)
conscious
correspondent

definite
dependent
design
devise (cf. device)
diminution
disappearance
dispel

effect (cf. affect)
embarrass
environment
exaggerate
existence

familiar
fascinate
flagrant
foreign
forth (cf. fourth)
fulfill *or* fulfil

government

harass

height
hindrance

incredible
independent
irresistible
its (cf. it's)

judgment

library
literature
lose (cf. loose)

maintenance (cf. maintain)
mathematics
minuscule
miracle
miscellaneous
mischief

necessary
neighbor
noticeable
nuisance

occasion
occurrence
occurred
offered
omitted

parallel
peculiar
possess

preceding (cf. proceeding)
prejudice
principal (cf. principle)
privilege

quite (cf. quiet)

receive
referring
relieve
remuneration
resemblance
reverence
ridiculous

seize
separate
similar
special
stationary (immobile)
stationery (paper)
succeed

than (cf. then)
their (cf. there)
threshold
too (cf. to)
tragedy
truly

usually

whose (cf. who's)
withhold

INDEX